A NATURALIST'S GUIDE TO THE

BUTTERFLIES
OF
BORNEO

Honor Phillipps

Photographs by
Honor Phillipps • Cosmo Phillipps

JOHN B

First published in the United Kingdom in 2024 by John Beaufoy Publishing Ltd
11 Blenheim Court, 316 Woodstock Road, Oxford OX2 7NS, England
www.johnbeaufoy.com

Photo captions and credits
Front cover: *main image* Blue Spotted Peacock © Honor Phillipps; *bottom left* Malayan Lacewing © Honor
Phillipps, *bottom centre* Cruiser © Honor Phillipps, *bottom right* Yellow Glassy Tiger © Honor Phillipps
Back cover: *Taraka hamada* on *Heliconia*, Crocker Range
Inside front cover: Skipper on banana plant
Inside back cover: Puddling butterflies
Title page: Common Mormon *Papilio polytes* (Maratua race) on Snakeweed
Contents page: Malayan Lacewing

All photographs are individually credited as follows: Cosmo Phillipps (CP), Honor Phillipps (HP)
and Quentin Phillipps (QP)

ISBN 978-1-906780-69-2

Edited by Krystyna Mayer
Designed by Nigel Partridge
Project management by Rosemary Wilkinson

Printed and bound in Malaysia by Times Offset (M) Sdn. Bhd.

·Contents·

LEPIDOPTERA PHYLOGENETIC TREE & QUICK REFERENCE KEY

Butterflies not shown to scale

LEPIDOPTERA

MOTHS p. 157
(Rama-rama)
125 families worldwide

BUTTERFLIES
(Kupu-kupu)
6 families worldwide

PAPILIONOIDEA

PAPILIONIDAE p. 28
- Birdwings & swallowtails
- Medium to very large
- Many are black with bright colours
  and showy patterns
- Some have paddle-shaped 'tails'

PIERIDAE p. 53
- Whites & yellows
- Small to medium
- Many with dark borders
- Some with boldly patterned underwings

NYMPHALIDAE p. 69
- A very large family including tigers, crows, pansies & sailors
- Of varied size
- Often bold colours and patterns, many with eyespots
- Underwings often camouflaged
- Only four functioning legs

▪ Family Tree ▪

HESPERIOIDEA

HESPERIIDAE p. 149
- Skippers
- Small
- Broad bodied, large head & eyes
- Dull colouring
- 'Moth-like'
- Hooked antennae

RIODINIDAE p. 138
- Metalmarks
- Small, bright and metallic

LYCAENIDAE p. 140
- Blues
- Small to medium
- Most have iridescent overwings and paler underwings with delicate markings
- Rest with wings closed (upright)
- Some have filamentous tails

INTRODUCTION

'You ask what is the use of butterflies', wrote John Ray (though his original text was in Latin). 'I reply, to adorn the world and delight the eyes of men: to brighten the countryside like so many golden jewels. To contemplate their exquisite beauty and variety is to experience the truest pleasure.' John Ray (1627–1705), Michael A. Salmon, *The Aurelian Legacy*, 2000.

There are currently approximately 19,750 species of butterfly in the world, grouped into six families. Of these, Borneo is home to approximately 1,000 species, many of which are shared with continental Southeast Asia, but Borneo also has a significant number of endemic species of its own. For its size, Borneo is very rich in butterfly species.

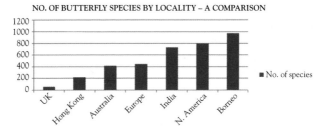

NO. OF BUTTERFLY SPECIES BY LOCALITY – A COMPARISON

The scope of the book The essential purpose of this guide is to help with identification of the 100 or so most common butterflies in Borneo. About 90 per cent of butterfly sightings are from this 10 per cent of the Bornean butterfly species.

Although the Lycaenidae (blues) and Hesperiidae (skippers) are most numerous, the most sightings are of Papilionidae (birdwings and swallowtails) Pieridae (whites and yellows) and Nymphalidae (tigers, pansies and so on), which are larger and showier butterflies. Therefore, a greater proportion of species from these families is included in the book. Some species with a particularly interesting ecology have extended entries.

There are also sections on the butterfly life cycle, butterfly morphology, habitats, nectar plants and larval food plants, and a section on moths.

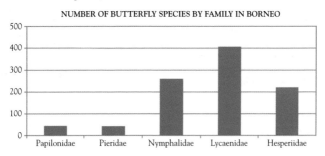

NUMBER OF BUTTERFLY SPECIES BY FAMILY IN BORNEO

Common names, alternative common names, if applicable, and scientific names are given for each butterfly, based on the previous literature. While common names may vary, scientific names are based on the original type description and are fixed from that date and universally recognized and accepted.

Wingspan is given for each species, defined as double the forewing length plus the body width and calculated by averaging data from relevant sources. The actual wingspan length is shown by the vertical red line with each species. This is not intended as definitive but is provided to give a sense of scale for people seeing the butterfly for the first time.

Photos of butterflies are all of the male – unless otherwise specified. If the female differs but no photo is available, then she is described in the text.

Abbreviations ♂ male, ♀ female. N north, S south, E east, W west, NW north-west, NE north-east, SW south-west and SE south-east.

Habitat Elevations are given as a rough guide only. Metres above sea level: m asl.

Specialist terms Those used in the book are highlighted as follows:

ENGLISH	SCIENTIFIC Singular	SCIENTIFIC Plural	MALAY Singular	Related adjective
Egg	Ovum	Ova	Telur	
Caterpillar	Larva	Larvae	Ulat	Larval
Chrysalis	Pupa	Pupae	Kepompong	Pupal
Adult	Imago	Imagines	Dewasa	

All the photographs were taken in the wild at various sites across Borneo, so that the butterflies are shown in their natural environments and in their natural settling posture.

Male butterflies take in salt to increase their fertility. Since they cannot obtain salt from plants – they turn to animal secretions, including urine, tears and sweat. Some species in particular are strongly attracted to human sweat, including *Anthene emolus*, *Vindula dejone* and many of the crows in the Nymphalidae. So, if you are feeling tired and hot after trekking through the forest in search of butterflies – do not despair. Sit down peacefully on a handy rock and if you are lucky the butterflies will come and find you.

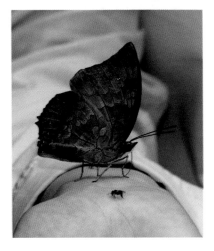

Charaxes bernardus is a fast-flying forest butterfly, one of several species that are strongly attracted to human sweat, Belalong River (QP)

■ CLIMATE & GEOGRAPHICAL REGIONS ■

CLIMATE

The temperature in lowland Borneo varies from c. 22°C at night to c. 32°C during the day. The temperature falls with altitude. Kinabalu Park HQ (1,500m asl) is c. 9°C cooler than at sea level. The abundance and variety of butterflies decreases with altitude. No Bornean butterfly breeds above 2,000m asl.

Rain falls almost every day throughout Borneo with a short dry season in Sabah from February–April. Adult butterflies are most abundant at the start of the dry season.

GEOGRAPHICAL REGIONS REFERRED TO IN THE TEXT

The island of Borneo – Sabah, Sarawak (states of Malaysia), Brunei (independent sultanate) and Kalimantan (district of Indonesia).

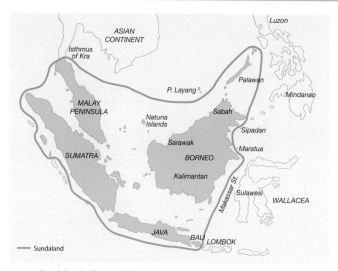

Sundaland – *Borneo, Malay peninsula, Sumatra, Java, Bali and Palawan.*

Oriental Region – *India (south of the Himalayas), South China, Myanmar (Burma), Thailand, Laos, Cambodia, Vietnam, Peninsular Malaysia, Borneo, Sumatra, Java, Bali, Philippines, Palawan, Ryukyu islands (Japan), Taiwan, Hong Kong and Hainan.*

Sites Referred to in Text

1. Kinabalu Park HQ – Gng Kinabalu
- Montane butterflies
- Numerous moths, many endemic
- Montane forest
- Birds include minivets, trogons and barbets
- www.mountkinabalu.com
- www.sabahtourism.com/destination/kinabalu-park

2. Kinabalu Park – Poring Hot Springs
- Butterfly garden
- Hill forest

- Waterfalls and hot springs
- Bathing pools
- Excellent information centre/ butterfly exhibition

3. Kota Kinabalu, Karambunai, Kokol Ridge
- Garden and open country butterflies

4. Sepilok Forest Reserve & Rainforest Discovery Centre
- Forest butterflies
- Lowland rainforest

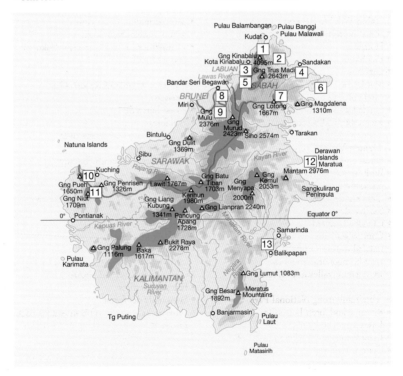

- Birds include Bristlehead and hornbills
- Orangutan Rehabilitation Centre
- Canopy walkway
- Excellent visitor centre
- Proboscis monkeys at nearby Labuk Bay
- www.forest.sabah.gov.my/rdc
- www.sabahtourism.com/destination/rainforest-discovery-centre-rdc

5. Kipandi Butterfly House & Gardens
- Exhibits of live larvae and pupae
- Butterfly and beetle museum
- Orchid house
- www.sabahtourism.com/destination/kipandi-butterfly-park

6. Tabin Wildlife Reserve
- Forest butterflies
- Hornbills
- Elephants
- Gibbons
- Macaques
- Mud volcano
- Guided walks
- www.tabinwildlife.com.my

7. Danum Valley Conservation Area
- Forest and riverine butterflies
- Birds include hornbills, pittas and pheasants
- Orangutans
- Sambar deer
- Clouded Leopard
- Canopy walkway
- Guided walks
- www.borneonaturetours.com (Lodge)
- www.danumvalley.info/ (Field Centre)

8. Ulu Temburong National Park
- Riverine and forest butterflies
- Interesting variety of moths
- Remote unspoilt lowland rainforest
- Canopy walkway
- www.uluuluresort.com

9. Mulu National Park
- Forest and open country butterflies
- River flood plain forest
- Birds include Bat Hawk and hornbills
- Bats
- Limestone caves
- Canopy walkway
- Excellent visitor centre and guided walks
- www.mulunationalpark.com

10. Bako National Park & Permai Resort
- Forest and seashore butterflies
- Coastal forest
- Macaques
- Wild pigs
- Smooth Otter
- www.permairainforest.com
- www.sarawakforestry.com
- sarawaktourism.com/attraction/bako-national-park

11. Borneo Highland Resort, Gng Penrissen
- Forest butterflies
- Hill forest
- Ridgetop path with views over Kalimantan
- www.borneohighlands.com.my

12. Maratua Island
- Island species of butterflies and birds
- Turtles
- Rare jellyfish
- Snorkelling
- www.maratua.com

13. Sungai Wain, Balikpapan
- Forest butterflies
- Seasonally dry forest
- Birds include pittas and Bornean peacock pheasant

THE BORNEAN ENVIRONMENT

'… the natural vegetation of Borneo is tropical rainforest.' (J. Payne, 1994).

SOME KEY DEFINITIONS

Tropical Rainforest The forests of the permanently wet tropics (Borneo average annual rainfall is 1,750mm), were originally defined by botanist A. F. W. Schimper in 1898 as 'evergreen, at least 30m tall, rich in thick-stemmed lianas and epiphytes'. The trees' branches form a continuous canopy, generally punctuated by the occasional 'emergent' (a single, taller tree). Many trees develop buttresses to compensate for shallow roots. The forest floor is home to ferns, gingers, begonias, other shade-tolerant plants and fungi. This vegetation (with fungi) is known as the understorey.

More than 3,000 tree species have been recorded in Borneo, and species of dipterocarp dominate the forest. The tree canopy is 40–70m tall, with emergent trees up to 75m or more. The forest contains a wide range of tree sizes, from spindly saplings to mature giants with trunks more than 3m in circumference, and occasional gaps created by tree fall. 'This variety in structure of the old growth forests is a key factor in maintaining the diversity of wildlife.' (J. Payne, 1994).

Primary Forest Forest that has remained undisturbed since it became established. Also known as climax forest. Having reached the apex of plant succession, the plant community becomes more or less self-perpetuating and further changes in the plant composition are minimal.

Any particular area of the Bornean forest may be a few thousand to tens of millions of years old – although it will have varied in plant species composition over time. Individual

Primary lowland/hill forest, Belalong, Brunei, CP

trees at their maturity may be 30 years old (Macaranga) to 1,000 years old (Belian, or Ironwood). The dipterocarp trees that make up the majority of the forest live to 200–300 years.

When a tree dies and crashes to the ground a clearing is formed. These clearings let in sun and form micro habitats that are often frequented by butterflies. Initially colonized by low herbaceous plants, eventually new trees grow up in these spaces. They are seeded from the surrounding trees, so the forest regenerates naturally.

Secondary Forest A forest growing on an area where original forest has been cleared or destroyed. It typically occurs along roadsides, on land adjacent to cultivated land, on landslips and in forest clearings. It is characteristically of lower stature, less dense and has a different mix of tree species.

Other Forest Types These include, for example, heath forest (kerangas), swamp forest, limestone forest, ultrabasic forest

Trees of the primary lowland forest, Danum, HP

and cloud forest of the upper montane reaches. Each has its own characteristics and more limited mix of plant species and butterfly species than the above forest types.

Open Country Unutilized cleared land is initially colonized by grasses, and later shrubs (typically of the Leguminosae, or pea family). Many of these shrubs are free-flowering plants that are attractive to butterflies for their nectar.

Butterflies fly where their larval food plants occur or where there are abundant nectar flowers. Butterfly species may be generalists or specialists associated with one particular plant and habitat. With regard to butterfly distribution, three broad habitats have been outlined by Corbet & Pendlebury (*The Butterflies of the Malay Peninsula*, 1934).

1. Lowland Open Country This includes gardens, in towns or villages, roadsides, scrubland, plantations and deserted forest clearings. About 10–12 per cent of Bornean butterfly species are to be found in this type of habitat.

2. Lowland to Hill Forest Up to around 750m altitude. The lowland primary rainforest is home to the vast majority of butterfly species occurring in Borneo. In the forest they may fly high in the canopy, in the understorey, in clearings, or along streams and rivers.

3. Hill to Montane Forest From around 750m and above. Regarding butterflies, species richness decreases with altitude but endemism increases. Fewer butterflies are found at higher altitudes but moths are more numerous.

LIFE CYCLE

The four stages of the life cycle occur in every butterfly species but details vary. Size and phase duration figures given here indicate the range of that variation across species.

EGG/OVUM
Size 0.4–2.1mm, phase duration 2–7 days.

Cycad Blue, Chilades pandava, on a cycad leaf, with eggs, Karambunai (CP)

The single, orange egg of the Black Rose, Pachliopta aristolochiae, Belalong (HP)

Each species of butterfly has a particular plant species or number of plant species on which its larvae are able to feed and thrive, known as the **larval food plant(s)** (p. 168). The tiny eggs are usually laid on a leaf, but sometimes on a stem or flower bud, and secured by an adhesive secreted by the female. The eggs are laid singly, or in small or large batches of up to several hundred, depending on the species. Some butterflies whose larvae feed on grasses fly over, scattering their eggs as they go. Eggs are generally green and thus well camouflaged in situ, but some are white, yellow, orange or red. They darken just before hatching into a larva. The **micropyle** – the spot where sperm enters and later the larva exits – is visible within the small depression at the top of each egg.

CATERPILLAR/LARVA
Final size 11–60mm, phase duration 6–37 days.

Mottled Emigrant, Catopsilia pyranthe, larva camouflaged on its food plant, Mulu (HP).

Malayan Eggfly, Hypolimnas anomala, the spiny, final instar larvae, Maratha (QP)

This is the main growth phase in the life cycle of a butterfly, generally sustained entirely by eating plant material, although some species are carnivorous. Larvae typically increase in weight by 1,000-fold or more. They go through 5–7 growth stages known as **instars** and at the end of each one their skin, which has become too tight, is shed; this is known as **ecdysis**. They may entirely change in appearance after each moult. Various strategies to avoid potential predators have evolved. Some larvae are green and well camouflaged on the food plant, others are toxic and have bright warning colours in black and red, orange or yellow; some have defensive spines, and others remain hidden in curled up leaves.

CHRYSALIS/PUPA
Size 7–45mm, phase duration 5–21 days

Twig-like pupa of the Lime butterfly, Papilio demoleus, *KNPHQ. (CP)*

Leaf-like pupa of the Common Birdwing, Troides helena, *Kipandi. (CP)*

Once a larva has reached full size it searches for a safe place to pupate, generally leaving the food plant in order to find a site hidden among foliage. Most larvae spin a silk pad on a twig or stem and attach themselves to this by tiny hooks at the tail end – known as the **cremaster**. Some species also spin a **silken girdle**. The skin splits open for the final time, revealing the pupa. The pupa is immobile and therefore vulnerable to both extremes of weather and predation, and most pupae are green or brown and well camouflaged. Inside the pupa metamorphosis takes place. The body of the larva is broken down and recreated in a new form – the adult butterfly. Once complete the pupal case splits open and the new butterfly emerges.

ADULT/IMAGO
Size (wingspan) 18–190mm, phase duration 5 days–10 weeks
The adult is the most conspicuous and widely known stage, although it often only lasts a short time. Wings enable flight in order to feed, find a mate and find a suitable egg-laying site, thus completing the life cycle.

Lacewing, Cethosia hypsea, *recently emerged from pupa, drying its wings, Kipandi (HP)*

Parts of a Butterfly

Apex

Forewing

Hindwing

Antennae

Palpi

Compound Eye

Proboscis

Thorax (contains muscles that power flight)

Furry Body

Scales cover the wings

Wing edge (scalloped, smooth, toothed, etc.)

Veins

Abdomen (contains digestive and reproductive organs)

Legs (3 pairs)

BELOW ARE ADDITIONAL FEATURES PRESENT IN SOME BUT NOT ALL BUTTERFLIES

Transverse band

Cilia (hairs)

Filamentous tails

Submarginal eyespots

Scent brands (male only)

Eyespot

THE PROBOSCIS

The proboscis is a long, flexible feeding tube formed from two lengthways pieces joined together down the centre by tiny hooks, which can be uncoupled if necessary for cleaning. The thick outer walls of the proboscis contain nerves and air ducts, as well as muscles that enable movement. Liquid nourishment, including nectar, sap and mineral-rich water, is sucked up the central channel by the use of powerful muscles in the butterfly's head. When not in use the proboscis is held coiled up in front of the butterfly's face.

Skipper butterfly (Hesperiidae)

Proboscis Length In general the length of the proboscis is roughly equivalent to the length of the butterfly's body.

This means that larger butterflies have a longer proboscis and can access nectar in flowers with deeper corollas and in many cases 'pollination syndromes' have evolved. However, the Hesperiidae (illustrated) have a disproportionately long proboscis – up to 2.5 times the body length. When they take nectar they do not necessarily pollinate the flower they visit and hence are known as 'nectar robbers'.

Nano Sponge While butterflies are often seen probing into flowers for nectar, or damp mud or sand for water, with the tip of their proboscis, they can also be seen with the latter part of the proboscis curved back towards themselves and simply laid flat on the moist

surface of rotting fruits. Recent research has shown that the physical structure of the lower length of the proboscis acts as a nanosponge and allows butterflies to draw up liquid by capillary action through the outer wall. 'The butterfly proboscis thus represents a sponge and a drinking straw in a single embodiment.' (Monaenkova, D. et al, 2011). This dual function has allowed the evolution of diverse feeding habits among butterflies, and some now feed exclusively on juices from over-ripe fruits.

WING STRUCTURE

Each wing consists of a framework of veins covered by an upperside and underside membrane with overlapping scales arranged in rows. The scales are responsible for the colours of the wings. The colour pattern on a butterfly's wing 'is in effect a finely tiled mosaic of monochrome scales' (Frederik H. Nijhout, 1991). The colours of the scales are due to either pigments that they contain, or are produced physically by reflection and diffraction of light caused by ridges on the scale surfaces. Additionally, males of many species have specialized scent scales called androconia, from which pheromones (scents) are emitted during courtship.

WING PATTERNS

All butterfly wing patterns are symmetrical (about the body) except for ripple patterns (such as the underwings of the Mottled Migrant), which are random and therefore different on the left and right wings. The multitude of various wing patterns has evolved from a limited number of elements. 'Each element appears to be able to change in evolution independently from the others, and it is the permutation of size, shape, colour, and presence or absence of this relatively small set of pattern elements that is responsible for much of the observed diversity of wing patterns in the butterflies and moths.' (Frederik H. Nijhout, 1991)

Pattern Functions Attracting a mate and mate recognition is one important and easily apparent function of the colours and patterns of butterflies' wings. Another essential purpose of various wing patterns is the avoidance or deterrence of predators, and the increase in survival chances. Some colouration and patterns allow a butterfly to remain undetected, while others act as a bold warning of unpalatability.

CAMOUFLAGE PATTERNS

Camouflage is the simplest form of mimicry. In this instance a butterfly's wing pattern mimics the surface on which it typically lands to rest or feed. Many forest butterflies have

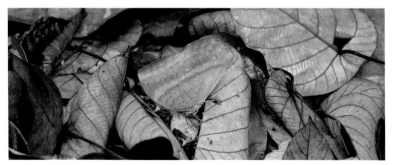

Blue Duffer, Discophora necho, *amongst fallen leaves, Mulu (HP)*

Great Oak Leaf, Kallima limborgi, *Poring (CP)*

wings coloured in shades of brown with subtle patterning to merge with fallen dead leaves on the forest floor. See preceding page for illustration showing the Blue Duffer.

Disguise Patterns In a similar manner, some butterflies mimic other objects in their environment. The Great Oak Leaf shown here, looks like a dead leaf and usually rests hanging from the branch of a tree among the real leaves. Effective disguise often also depends on settling posture. See also the Broken Twig Moth (p. 162).

Disruptive Colouration Some butterflies have a disjointed wing pattern that breaks up the outline shape of the butterfly, making it difficult for a predator to see. The Banded Blue Pierrot shown here, frequents gravel-stream beds. A closely related species, the Elbowed Pierrot (p. 141), spends time in dappled shade on the ground at the forest edge. In both habitats the butterfly is difficult to make out at a distance. Additionally, at close proximity the black and white act as warning colours (see below).

Banded Blue Pierrot, Discolampa ethion, *on gravel shore, Mulu (HP)*

Banded Blue Pierrot, Discolampa ethion, *close up, Tabin (HP)*

Grey Glassy Tiger, Ideopsis juventa, *Karambunai (HP)*

Aposematic/Warning Colours The larvae of some species feed on plants containing toxins that they sequester (retain without digesting), making the adult butterfly unpalatable to potential predators such as birds or lizards. In order to deter predator attacks these butterflies have evolved conspicuous warning colouration signalling their unpalatability. The colours are typically red, orange, yellow or white, very often in combination with black, frequently in a striking striped pattern. Butterflies with warning colouration have no fear of attack, and are often easier to photograph.

Diematic Patterns Some wing patterns in butterflies have evolved to startle or scare potential predators. The most common are large, bold eyespots that give the impression of eyes belonging to a much larger animal. This is particularly effective in dim light conditions such as those deep in dappled shade. A predator may retreat altogether or at the least be startled long enough to allow the butterfly to fly away.

After analysis of the border wing patterns of 2,207 species across 321 genera of Nymphalidae, evolutionary biologist Frederik H. Nijhout found that the most common shape to have evolved, occurring in 651 of the species, was the fully formed 'eyespot' or ocellus.

Utang Resident, Coelites euptychoides, *Sungai Wain (HP)*

Common Three Ring, Ypthima pandocus, *Karambunai (HP)*

Decoy Patterns Predators usually attack the head of their prey first, particularly the eyes. Conspicuous eyespot markings found on the outer edges of butterfly wings in many species are known to act as a decoy to divert predator attack away from the real head. This individual shows evidence of a bite taken out of its hindwing (see right).

False Head Illusion Decoy markings reach the greatest sophistication in the Lycaenidae butterflies, creating the illusion of a false head.
The four main components of this deception are an eyespot at the tip on the underside of the hindwing, thread-like

Lilac-banded Bush Brown, Mycalesis oroatis, *Poring (CP)*

Chocolate Royal, Remelana jangala, *Sungai Wain (HP)*

Spindaris *spp. Maliau (HP)*

tails (mimicking antennae), an unusually sharp angle to the hindwing, and converging contrasting lines that act to draw attention to the false eye. The hindwing may terminate in a flattened lobe with white highlights appearing like a head. Entomologist Robert Robbins (1981) found that species with all four elements present were five times more likely to escape a predator's attack than those with only two. The more complete the deception, the greater the protection. The attacker gets only a mouthful of wing.

The deception of a false head may be enhanced by a butterfly's behaviour, including moving the tails subtly to simulate antennae movement and turning to face head down on landing in a vertical or near-vertical position, so presenting the false head uppermost where the predator would expect the head to be.

MIMICRY

Batesian Mimicry While all butterflies that are toxic to predators display warning colouration, not all butterflies that display warning colours are in fact unpalatable.

Henry Walter Bates, an entomologist, while exploring South America in 1848, observed that some butterflies of a species that he knew to be palatable (the mimics) had evolved to look exactly like butterflies of an unpalatable species (the models) that occurred in the same area. He rightly concluded that this resemblance gave the mimics protection from predators who, seeing the warning colouration, would back off. He was the first to record this phenomenon and in consequence it is known as 'Batesian mimicry'.

Striped Blue Crow, Euploea mulciber, *Temburong – the mimic (HP)*

Cyclosia midama *– a day-flying moth, Maliau – the model (HP)*

Müllerian Mimicry In some instances, several different sympatric species of unpalatable butterfly have evolved the same warning colour pattern, known as a 'mimicry ring'. This benefits all species in the ring as it reinforces the warning signal to potential predators while reducing the number of predator attacks on each individual species. This is known as Müllerian mimicry after Fritz Müller, who first described the phenomenon in 1878.

FLASH COLOURATION
A few forest butterflies have dull underwings but iridescent upperwings, so that when they fly they give the appearance of a light flashing on and off, making it very confusing for a predator to follow. Once they settle with only the subdued underwing showing, they merge into the forest background again instantly. Examples are the Jungle Glory butterflies.

POLYMORPHISM
A butterfly species can occur in several different forms, for example, in the Great Mormon species the female has evolved various forms to mimic different toxic butterflies and is thus protected from predation. By mimicking several different models, the likelihood of the mimics outnumbering the models is reduced, thus conferring a higher chance of survival on the individual, and ultimately, the species.

DIMORPHISM
In many species of butterfly the male and female look the same and are indistinguishable in the field (other than possibly by behaviour). In some species the male may be distinguished only by the presence of a 'scent brand' (p. 17). Males may also have more elongated wings that enable faster, more manoeuvrable flight, whereas females have more rounded wings. However, in some species the male and female do look different. This is known as gender dimorphism or sexual dimorphism. In many cases of gender dimorphism the differences are limited and subtle. In a few species, such as the Cruiser, shown here, the male and female look like entirely different species. The female Cruiser is well camouflaged as she moves high among the trees in the dappled light at the forest edge, finding a suitable vine to lay her eggs on, while the male is protected by warning colouring as he takes up mineral-rich water on nearby open muddy ground.

Cruiser ♀, Vindula dejone, *Karambunai (HP)*   *Cruiser* ♂, Vindula dejone, *Sungai Wain (HP)*

Behaviour

FLYING

Butterflies spend a large proportion of each day in flight, weather permitting, and it is then that they are most noticeable. Flight is essential as a means of finding three vital resources: food, mates and host plants. It is also important as a means of escaping predator attack, and in some instances, for migration.

A Skipper (Hesperiidae) taking flight, Sungai Wain forest (HP)

Flight is driven by powerful muscles in the thorax. The wings flap, bend and twist in complex ways to enable control as well as movement. '… it is better to compare a butterfly wing with a sail, rather than the fixed wing of an aeroplane or the muscular wing of a bird' (Dick Vane-Wright, *Butterflies*, 2003). Flight may be high up or low, swift and direct, or slow and fluttering, depending on the species and circumstance.

Different butterfly groups are often associated with different flight styles. Most swallowtails (papilionids) use a half-hovering movement when at flowers taking nectar. Most yellow butterflies (pierids) have a characteristic fluttering, haphazard flight. Many of the nymphalids have a powerful flap-and-glide style. Skippers (hesperiids) have a fast, direct flight and are particularly adept at vertical take-off. Nonetheless, most butterflies adapt their flight mode to the circumstances.

> Butterflies flap their wings at a rate of between about five beats per second in the swallowtails, and up to about 20 beats per second in the skippers. 'Some butterflies can sustain forward flight for hours, travelling 100km (60 miles) in a day … while sprint speeds of 30km per hour (20 miles per hour) or more are reached by certain butterflies, which places them … amongst the fastest of all flying insects.' (Dick Vane-Wright, *Butterflies*, 2003).

DISPERSAL & MIGRATION

Dispersal This is a flight undertaken by individual butterflies away from the site where they emerge. Butterflies are programmed to disperse and colonize new areas under certain conditions. Environmental triggers include insufficient abundance of the larval food plant, changes in climate and insufficient numbers of potential mates. Journeying butterflies will stop when they find the first suitable new location and rarely travel more than a few kilometres from the initial site. Dispersing butterflies will also meet and mate with butterflies from other source colonies, thus avoiding unfavourable levels of inbreeding.

Migration This involves long-distance directional movement and unlike dispersal is a two-way process, with one generation flying on the outward journey and the offspring of a later generation making the return. The numbers involved are often in the tens of thousands, sometimes millions, on the outward migration but are always much lower on the return. How migrating butterflies navigate is not entirely understood, but it seems that they utilize a mixture of instinct, orienting by the sun and the Earth's magnetic field. The Lemon Migrant is the best-known example of butterfly migration in Southeast Asia.

FEEDING

'The diet of a butterfly is of necessity a liquid one' (d'Abrera, 2005), the chewing mouthparts of the larva (caterpillar) having been replaced

A Skipper (Hesperiidae) feeding on a banana flower, Mulu (HP)

with adapted mouthparts in the form of a long, thin tube called a proboscis (see p. 18).

In most butterfly species the main source of food, and thereby energy, is nectar from flowers, both wild and cultivated (p. 170), with a preference for flowers that produce nectar that is composed of 20–25 per cent sugars. However, many butterflies also feed on juices exuded from over-ripe fruit, or sap oozing from tree trunks, or (aphid) honeydew, and for some forest species these may be the main source of nutrition.

Butterflies, particularly males, also extract essential salts and minerals from animal sweat, urine and excrement, bird droppings, rotting animal carcasses, ash from fires and damp concrete.

PUDDLING

Drinking from damp ground, singly or in groups, is known as 'puddling'. To absorb requisite chemicals in sufficient quantities from dilute sources, such as puddles or stream edges, without becoming waterlogged, fluid may be squirted out through the anus intermittently while drinking.

BASKING & THERMOREGULATION

In order to take flight and become active, a butterfly must reach the critical body temperature of approximately 25°C or more. As butterflies cannot generate their own body heat they are dependent on the ambient temperature. Although in Borneo the typical lowland daytime temperature is 26–32°C, butterflies still need to warm up in the early morning after night-time temperatures as low as 22°C, after rain, and in mountainous areas where the temperature is about 10 degrees cooler than in the lowlands. In order to warm up, a butterfly moves to a prominent perch such as a large, flat leaf in full sunshine, then basks.

The effectiveness of basking can be improved by choosing a substrate on which to bask, such as stone, bare earth, wood or metal, which reflects heat upwards to the body. To cool down in the heat of the day butterflies can adjust their body posture to minimize heating from the sun, or move to a cooler place out of the direct sunlight. With these adjustments they can regulate their own body temperature.

DIFFERENT SPECIES EMPLOY DIFFERENT STRATEGIES AND POSTURES:
'**Dorsal-basking**' **species** (many nymphalids) rest with their wings outspread flat in the direct sun, warming the air trapped between their wings and the surface on which they rest, which in turn transfers heat to their body.
'**Lateral-basking**' **species** (many lycaenids) sit with their wings held upright over the body, broadside to the direction of the sun's rays, allowing the side of the body to be warmed directly.
'**Reflectance-basking**' **species** (many pierids) have pale, highly reflective upperwing surfaces and sit with their wings partially open, in a wide 'V' shape, so that the sun is reflected off the wings down on to the body, thus warming it.

COURTSHIP & MATING

Mating consists of three essential stages – mate location, courtship and copulation. Males use either of two different key strategies for locating a mate, widely known as 'perching' and 'patrolling'. Which is used depends largely on the larval host plant used.

In the case of larger host plants, such as trees, or a concentrated patch of smaller host plants, the male establishes a territory close to the host plant in anticipation of females of a previous generation emerging from their pupal phase ready to be mated, or hoping to encounter wandering females.

Perching males take up a prominent vantage point within their perceived 'territory' and wait there for a female to fly nearby, whereupon they will fly out to intercept her. If a male

A pair of Multi Palmfly, Elymnias penanga, *mating,♀ on the left, Poring (HP)*

A pair of Eurema mating, Tanjung Aru (QP)

of the same species flies near he is chased off, but individuals of other species are tolerated.

Alternatively, if the larval host plant is small and widely scattered, males fly large distances, '**patrolling**' tirelessly over grassy areas, through forests, along tracks or streams, wherever the host plant grows, in the hope of encountering a female.

Courtship rituals vary from species to species, but often involve an aerial chase followed by swirling around each other. Once grounded again the male usually approaches the female tentatively, sometimes releasing pheromones from special scent scales on his wings. If already mated or if sensing him inadequate, the female can refuse him by adopting a rejection posture that makes copulation impossible.

Copulation takes place end to end facing away from each other and the pair remains engaged for several minutes to several hours, depending on the species. During this time the male transfers a sperm package to the female and often also a package of nutrients. If disturbed during copulation they will fly off still conjoined, with the flight powered by the female. After copulation the female seeks a suitable host plant (or host plants) on which to lay her eggs, and the male may well seek to mate again with another female.

Egg Laying Each butterfly species has a particular species of plant, or sometimes several plants, on which the larvae can feed and thrive. Once successfully mated, the female flies in search of a suitable plant(s) of the correct species on which to lay her eggs, which may be laid singly or in batches.

The host plant should ideally be in good condition, young and healthy, not on a main thoroughfare where it may be grazed or trampled, and not already carrying eggs of another butterfly whose larvae would compete for food.

The female initially locates the plant by sight, then confirms her identification and tests for condition with the use of chemical receptors in her feet. A butterfly that repeatedly lands on a plant or number of plants and takes off again, but is apparently not feeding, is probably a female probing for a suitable host plant. If she stays a bit longer and curls her abdomen around to make contact with the plant, she is probably laying her eggs.

A ♀ Black Rose, Pachliopta aristolochiae *laying her eggs, Belalong forest (HP)*

Rajah Brooke's Birdwing ■ *Trogonoptera brookiana* (Wallace, 1855)
(Borneo race – *brookiana*)

HABITAT Primary forest.   **ABUNDANCE** Moderately common.

♂ *Danum (CP)*

DESCRIPTION Sexes differ. Striking and unmistakable. Large birdwing with elongated forewings. Iridescent emerald green in a serrated band runs the length of forewing, on a velvet black background. Bright red collar. Female is paler than the male, with whitish feathery streaks towards the forewing-tip and white flecks along the hindwing margin (♀ shown below).

♀ *Temburong canopy walkway (40m) (QP)*

HABITAT AND HABITS Found along or near forest streams at all elevations. Strong in flight. Males may be seen flying purposefully through the trees or in the open along a ridge top or a forest road. Males also habitually congregate on moist paths, on riverbanks or near hot springs. Females generally fly in the canopy at 15m or more above ground level and deep in the forest, so are rarely seen. When they do appear, they occur singly. Breeds all year round. Common at Temburong and Mulu; also seen at Danum, Poring and Kinabalu Park HQ.

LARVAL FOOD PLANT Aristolochiaceae (birthwort family), *Aristolochia tagala* (climbing vine similar to Dutchman's Pipe), rare and widely dispersed (see below).

RANGE Borneo, Malay Peninsula, Sumatra and Natuna Islands.

ALFRED RUSSEL WALLACE, A MAGNIFICENT DISCOVERY AND AN INCONSPICUOUS VINE

Aristolochia tagala, a climbing vine, or liana, found in primary forest, is the food plant of the Raja Brooke's Birdwing's caterpillar. The larvae feed on the leaves but the flower is also shown here for identification purposes. Individual leaves grow to about 15cm in length and the vine climbs up tall forest trees to 50m or more in height. The leaves contain toxins that the larvae sequester, making both the larvae and subsequently the adult butterfly distasteful to potential predators.

Alfred Russel Wallace, 1823–1913, was of Welsh nationality. He initially trained as a surveyor but was interested in wildlife, particularly insects, from an early age. In 1848 he undertook a four- year collecting expedition to Brazil with friend and fellow naturalist Henry Walter Bates. Wallace travelled east to explore Southeast Asia in 1854 and collected countless scientific specimens over the following eight years, visiting many remote islands in the Malay archipelago. Wallace introduced the idea of gradual evolution due to the 'survival of the fittest' in a paper read to the Linnaean Society on his behalf on 1 July 1858. He was the first to observe and record the divide between the Asian and Australian biological regions – now known as Wallace's Line. Returning to Britain in 1862, he published *The Malay Archipelago*, his account of his travels, in 1869. He published many further scientific papers and lived in good health until the age of 90. He wrote that:

> My collection of butterflies was not large; but I obtained some rare and very handsome insects, the most remarkable being the *Ornithoptera Brookeana* [*Trogonoptera Brookiana*], one of the most elegant species known … This species, which was then quite new and which I named after Sir James Brooke, was very rare.

Common Birdwing ■ *Troides helena* (Linnaeus, 1758)
(Borneo race – *mosyclus*)

HABITAT Lowland to highland, forested areas.   **ABUNDANCE** Moderately common.

♂ *Kipandi (CP)*

DESCRIPTION Sexes differ. Large, with female larger than male. Male has entirely black forewing. Hindwing yellow with black scalloped border and black veins, and in Bornean subspecies a single isolated submarginal black spot near hind tip. Female has black forewing with broad, pale interveinal streaks. Her yellow hindwing additionally has an entire row of prominent black submarginal spots inner to the scalloped border. Variable. This is the most common and widespread of the birdwing species across the Oriental region, where 17 subspecies have been described so far.

SIMILAR SPECIES One of four similar species of Yellow Birdwing that occur in Borneo. Smaller than the most common, the Golden Birdwing (opposite).

HABITAT AND HABITS Found in forest clearings and along sunlit margins of the forest but also visits nearby open areas, including villages and gardens. Flies high in the canopy. Visits flowers for nectar and can be seen at tall flowering trees, but sometimes descends to flowering bushes. Unlike some Papilionidae, males *Troides* butterflies are not found at moist ground. Capable of flying long distances.

LARVAL FOOD PLANT Aristolochiaceae (Birthwort family); widely recorded on *Aristolochia acuminata*, *A. tagala* and *A. foveolata*.

RANGE N India east to SE China, Hainan, Hong Kong, south to Malay Peninsula, Singapore, Borneo, Sulawesi, Sumatra, Java and east to Sumbawa.

♀ *Poring (HP)*

Golden Birdwing ■ *Troides amphrysus* (Cramer, 1779)
(Borneo race – *flavicollis*) [Malayan Birdwing]

HABITAT Lowland to hill forest.   **ABUNDANCE** Moderately common.

DESCRIPTION
Sexes dissimilar.
Male large, female
larger. Very
variable. Above,
male has yellow
hindwing with
minimal continuous
wavy black border.
Forewing black,
usually with
distinct yellow
streaks along veins
but sometimes
white streaks or
none. Above,
female has yellow

♂ *Kipandi (CP)*

hindwing heavily darkened with thick, wavy border and inner row of large, conjoined
black spots forming a band. Female forewing largely pale grey-white with interveinal black
streaks. In some individuals the basal area is smudged dark brown.

SIMILAR SPECIES The largest of four yellow and black birdwings that occur in
Borneo, including the Common Birdwing (opposite). Male distinguished by minimal,
discontinuous hindwing border and pale streaking on forewing, female by dark-streaked
pale forewings. Also distinguished by greater size.

HABITAT AND HABITS Occurs in forest from the lowlands to hills. Found in sunnier
locations such as clearings,
along rivers and streams, and
at the forest edge. Generally,
flies high in the canopy.
Visits flowers for nectar. Rests
on leaves with wings open.
LARVAL FOOD PLANT
Aristolochiaceae, *Aristolochia
tagala, A. foveolata.*
RANGE S Myanmar and
S Thailand, to Malay
Peninsula, Sumatra, Java,
Borneo and Palawan.

♀ *Kipandi (HP)*

Black Rose ■ *Pachliopta aristolochiae* (Fabricius, 1775)
(Borneo race – *antiphus*) [Common Rose]

HABITAT Lowlands, forest, scrub, farms, islands.   **ABUNDANCE** Moderately common.

♀ *Maratua Island, Kalimantan (HP)*

DESCRIPTION
Sexes similar. Above entirely dusky black except for pale interveinal streaks on outer part of forewing and submarginal row of faint reddish crescents on hindwing. Underside similar to above but red crescents more prominent. Paddle (spatulate) tails. Head, sides of body and tip of abdomen bright red but less so in female than in male. Forewing more rounded in female. Throughout most of its range, apart from Borneo, has a white patch on the under hindwing (see box below).

SIMILAR SPECIES Mimicked by one form of the female of the non-toxic Common Mormon *Papilio polytes*, which, however, has no red on the body.

HABITAT AND HABITS Found in lowland forest where the larval food plant grows, but also frequents sunlit areas of nearby secondary vegetation, often near farms and villages,

P. aristolochiae - race: asteris, resident in Malay Peninsula and Singapore with white patch on underwing (Singapore, HP)

where it visits flowers for nectar. Restless, fluttering slowly over low vegetation, but if disturbed capable of great speed. Occasionally rests on a prominent leaf, its bright red and black warning colours deterring potential predators. Often found in small colonies. A known migrant and commonly occurs on larger offshore islands.

LARVAL FOOD PLANT Aristolochiaceae (birthwort family), recorded on both *Aristolochia*, including *A. tagala*, and *Thottea* species.

RANGE India and Sri Lanka, to S China, Taiwan, Ryukyu Islands, south to Malay Peninsula, Singapore, Borneo, Palawan, Philippines, Sumatra, Java, Bali to Flores.

WINGSPAN 84—94mm

Lime Butterfly ■ *Papilio demoleus* (Linnaeus, 1758)
(Borneo races – *malayanus*, *libanius*)

HABITAT Cultivated areas.   **ABUNDANCE** Locally common.

DESCRIPTION Sexes similar. Predominantly black above with extensive pattern of cream spots and patches, some of which form an irregular band down centre of wings. Known as the Chequered Swallowtail in Australia but lacks tails. Male has large, prominent red spot capped with blue and black at hindwing-tip, and in female this

Kipandi (HP)

is developed into a full eyespot. Underside cream with black and orange markings in a checked pattern.

HABITAT AND HABITS Flies very swiftly, preferring sunshine and open habitats generally at lower elevations. Common in gardens farms and villages and wherever citrus plants are cultivated. Habitually settles at edges of puddles to drink from the moist ground. Visits flowers for nectar.

LARVAL FOOD PLANT Rutaceae, especially *Citrus* spp., including the Kalamansi Lime, Lemon and Pomelo. Also recorded on Leguminosae (pea family) in India, Malay Peninsula, the Philippines and Australia.

RANGE Eastern Arabia, Iran, India, Sri Lanka, S China to Taiwan, south to the Philippines, Malay Peninsula, Sumatra and Borneo. Also New Guinea and E Australia to Hawaii.

First recorded in Borneo in 1976 at Tenom (Hill et al.) and on Mantanani Island (Robinson). Its previous absence from Borneo as well as Sumatra, Java and Sulawesi – despite occurring in adjacent Southeast Asia to the north-west and Australia to the south-east – remains a puzzle. It is known to be migratory in Australia. In Hong Kong it is the only *Papilio* found commonly on many of the small islands.

Kipandi (HP)

Black and White Helen ■ *Papilio nephelus* (Boisduval, 1836)
(Borneo race – *albolineatus*)

HABITAT Lowlands to hills, forest edge.   **ABUNDANCE** Moderately common.

Danum (CP)

DESCRIPTION
Sexes similar. Large, predominantly black butterfly with a distinct white band across the forewing and a large, irregular, triangular white patch across the hindwing. Broad, paddle-shaped (spatulate) tails to hindwings sometimes missing due to predator attack. Under hindwing has series of white or buff crescents along margin. Occurs in several races across the region. Some have little or no white on forewing, and others have yellowish crescents on under hindwing. Intermediate forms occur.

SIMILAR SPECIES One of eight species of black and white, tailed Papilio in Borneo, but the only one with a distinct white transverse band across forewing.

HABITAT AND HABITS Flies strongly and swiftly at moderate height in the open,

preferring sunlit sites near the forest edge by streams or rivers. Visits flowers for nectar and flies considerable distances even across open terrain to do so. Often comes to Ixora flowers at Danum lodge and Hibiscus flowers along Tabin lodge boardwalk. Males visit damp ground.

LARVAL FOOD PLANT Rutaceae (citrus family).

RANGE N India east to S China, Taiwan south to Malay Peninsula, Sumatra, Java and Borneo.

Mulu (HP)

Red Helen ■ *Papilio helenus* (Linnaeus, 1758)
(Borneo race – *enganius*)

HABITAT Forested areas, by rivers.

ABUNDANCE Moderately common.

WINGSPAN 115–122mm

DESCRIPTION Sexes similar, with female larger and paler than male. Large. Predominantly black with paddle (spatulate) tails. Above, hindwing has a three-segmented white patch and single red crescent (two in female) on inner margin at base of tail. Underside similar but with three large red rings next to base of tail. Row of three red crescents along hindwing outer margin (more in female than in male), sometimes very faint and, rarely, absent.

SIMILAR SPECIES One of the most common of several black and white *Papilio* species. Distinguished by row of red crescents along margin of underside of hindwing. Note that the near identical *P. iswaroides* is rarer and mostly montane.

HABITAT AND HABITS Found in

Danum (HP)

forested areas at all elevations, generally along streams and rivers, but most common in lowland forest at forest edge. Also in nearby farms and villages. Rapid, weaving flight. Flies in full sunshine, visiting flowers for nectar, particularly *Ixora* and *Clerodendron* spp. (p. 170). Males visit damp ground.

LARVAL FOOD PLANT Rutaceae (citrus family. Feeds on *Citrus* leaves, equally wild plants in the forest understorey and cultivated ones such as limes.

RANGE India, Sri Lanka, east to S China, Hong Kong, Taiwan, Japan, south through the Philippines, Southeast Asia mainland to Malay Peninsula, Borneo, Sumatra, Java, east to Timor.

Danum, on Ixora (HP)

Great Mormon ■ *Papilio memnon* (Linnaeus, 1758)
(Borneo race – *memnon*)

HABITAT Lowlands to hills, forest edge, gardens.   **ABUNDANCE** Moderately common.

Mulu (HP)

DESCRIPTION Sexes differ. Large. No tails. Male very dark blue-black with iridescent azure-blue scaling along hindwing veins above. Underneath a bright red patch at base of forewing (a red epaulette) is distinctive, and a double row of large black spots set in a greyish patch is faintly visible along hindwing border. Female polymorphic (occurs in several different forms). All forms have distinctive red patch at base of forewing above. The species is well known for the polymorphism of the female and her ability to evolve in order to mimic locally occurring toxic butterflies, conferring the benefit of a high survival rate. If the toxic models become extinct the mimetic forms decline, but may be replaced by the mimicking of new models.

HABITAT AND HABITS Strong flier and flies in the open, preferring full sunshine. Previously considered a rare jungle butterfly, but with the increasing cultivation of citrus plants, the food plant of its larvae, it has become a fairly common species of gardens and cultivation. Both male and female come to flowers to feed, and preferred nectar sources include *Ixora*, *Clerodendron* and *Citrus* (p. 170). The forewings are fluttered ceaselessly while feeding but the hindwings remain still.

LARVAL FOOD PLANT Rutaceae; *Citrus* spp. Larvae apparently prefer large-leaved kind of citrus, such as pomelo.

RANGE NE India east to Taiwan and S Japan south through Southeast Asia, Malay Peninsula, Singapore, to Sumatra, Java, Borneo, lesser Sunda Isles to Alor and Christmas Island.

WINGSPAN 14(-15)mm

♂ *Danum (HP)*

♀ *Kipandi (HP)*

♀ *Poring (CP)*

Bornean Mormon ■ *Papilio acheron* (Grose-Smith, 1887) **Endemic** (e)

HABITAT Hills, edge of forest.   **ABUNDANCE** Local.

WINGSPAN 105–115mm

DESCRIPTION Male all dark above with brownish-black forewings; hindwings blue-black with silvery scales in a broad band on the outer half. Underside dark purple-brown with red spot at base of hindwing and prominent gold patch at tail end containing three large black spots. Female has two forms. One resembles male but has paler ground colour and all three black spots well defined. The other has paler outer half of forewing.

SIMILAR SPECIES Similar to the closely related and more abundant Great Mormon (opposite).

Poring (HP)

Distinguished from male Great Mormon by smaller size, lack of interveinal streaks on hindwing above, and underneath, the distinctive gold patch and red basal spot confined to hindwing, and from any female Great Mormon by complete lack of any red marking on upperside.

HABITAT AND HABITS Inhabits forested areas at moderate elevations. Male flies fast and purposefully in sunlit areas habitually along streams, and comes to wet ground to drink, where it settles often for several minutes, opening and closing its forewings rapidly while drinking. Female keeps more to the forest.

LARVAL FOOD PLANT Rutaceae (citrus and rue family). Familiar as cultivated plants grown for fruits; in the tropics many species grow wild in the forest understorey.

RANGE Endemic to Borneo.

Poring (HP)

Blue Spotted Peacock ■ *Papilio karna* (C. & R. Felder, 1865)
(Borneo race – *carnatus*) [Jungle Jade]

HABITAT Lowland to hills, forested areas.   **ABUNDANCE** Not common, local.

Mulu (HP)

WINGSPAN 133mm

DESCRIPTION When Major C. M. Enriquez visited Borneo in 1925 on a scientific collecting expedition to the foothills and mountain of Kinabalu, he wrote: 'All the splendour with which butterflies are endowed seems to be developed in this beauty. It has a span of 5¼ inches; the fore-wings, the upper half of the hind-wing, and the superb swallow-tails being black, richly peppered over with a green frost. Across the centre of the hind-wing is a blaze of peacock-blue, with violet and purple reflections according to the light … Nothing could possibly be more splendid.'

SIMILAR SPECIES The Banded Peacock *P. palinurus* is smaller and has a broad blue band across the forewing above. Also note that the very similar *P. paris* occurs from India east to S China and Taiwan, and south to Sumatra and Java, but not in Borneo.

HABITAT AND HABITS Most common in the west. Found from the lowlands to the hills, from forest edge to villages, preferring sunny sites. Visits flowers for nectar. Swift and powerful in flight, usually flying high up but may flash past lower down in a tantalizing blaze of colour. Occasionally found resting with wings spread on a low leaf in full sun. The male takes up water from wet ground, sometimes as part of a congregation.

LARVAL FOOD PLANT Rutaceae (rue and citrus family).

RANGE Borneo, Sumatra, Java and Palawan.

Mulu (HP)

Common Bluebottle ■ *Graphium sarpedon* (Linnaeus, 1758)

(Borneo race – *sarpedon*) [Blue Triangle]

HABITAT Lowlands, forested areas.   **ABUNDANCE** Moderately common.

DESCRIPTION Sexes similar. Broad, translucent blue-green band tapering at the extremities traverses centre of both wings, appearing turquoise to sea-green depending on the light. Band fragments to large spots towards forewing apex. Otherwise ground colour black above, dark brown below. Hindwing underneath has a few scattered, small red streaks within the dark border. Wings slender and pointed.

SIMILAR SPECIES The most common of seven similar species in the same genus. Distinguished by almost entirely unbroken central band of blue-green and lack of any pale bluish spots within the dark forewing margin.

HABITAT AND HABITS Prefers open, sunny spaces in and around forests. Often active throughout the hottest part of the day. Restless. Easily disturbed. Flies very swiftly and alights abruptly. Males can be seen at puddles or damp patches singly or in loose groups along sandy or muddy riverbanks or on gravel rural roads. Visits flowers.

LARVAL FOOD PLANT Lauraceae (avocado and cinnamon family); also Annonaceae (sweetsop and soursop family), Magnoliaceae (magnolia family).

RANGE From India through southern China, to Japan, Taiwan and south through the Philippines, Southeast Asia, Malay Peninsula, Singapore, Borneo, Sumatra, Java, east to the Solomon Islands and south to E Australia.

Temburong (CP)

WINGSPAN 74–84mm

Red Spot Bluebottle ■ *Graphium doson* (C&R Felder, 1864)

(Borneo races – *evemonides*, *sarpedonoides*) [Common Jay]

HABITAT Lowlands, forested areas, larger islands.   **ABUNDANCE** Moderately common.

Danum, roadside (CP)

DESCRIPTION Sexes similar above. Above, broad blue central panel to both wings, and submarginal row of large blue spots contrasting with heavy black border. Underneath the same pattern but paler, washed-out blue on brown and with red flecks in hindwing border. Male has long brown hairs on inner margin of hindwing, hard to see in the field.

SIMILAR SPECIES One of seven very similar species. Distinguished by conspicuous red dot positioned on short black separate bar near base of hindwing on underside, visible when settled.

HABITAT AND HABITS Flies swiftly in open, sunlit spaces within forested areas. Enjoys full sunshine and active throughout midday. Males often seen at damp patches along gravelly forest roads, or sipping water from muddy ditches or riverbanks, singly or in company of others. Takes flight every couple of minutes, settling again nearby. Female is slower, keeps more to the forest and visits flowers for nectar.

LARVAL FOOD PLANT Lauraceae (avocado and cinnamon family), Magnoliaceae (magnolia family), Annonaceae (soursop family), *Polyalthia* spp.

RANGE From India, Sri Lanka, through S China, to S Japan, Taiwan, the Philippines, south to Malay Peninsula, Singapore (Pulau Ubin), Sumatra, Java, Borneo, and east to Sumbawa.

WINGSPAN 74–84mm

Blue Jay ■ *Graphium evemon* (Boisduval, 1836)
(Borneo race – *orthia*) [Lesser Jay]

HABITAT Lowland forest, by rivers.   **ABUNDANCE** Only locally common.

DESCRIPTION Sexes similar. Central wing panel of vibrant blue above, with a series of large blue submarginal spots set in a black border. Underside broadly the same, but more subdued, with paler blue, and hindwing yellow tinged at base and has red flecks in border.

SIMILAR SPECIES One of seven very similar species distinguished by the black bar along the lower margin on the underside of the hindwing, which forms a distinct 'Y' shape and contains no red spot.

HABITAT AND HABITS Found in forested areas in the lowlands. Frequents sandy river shores, where it 'puddles' for hours, probing the sand for moisture enriched by animal urine, or stands among small pebbles at the shallow water's edge sipping water directly from the river. Usually in the company of others, often of the same species. Active throughout the midday sun. Flight swift. In Borneo and Malay Peninsula considered uncommon, but common in Singapore.

LARVAL FOOD PLANT No records in Borneo. In Singapore, Annonaceae (soursop family), *Artabotrys*; Lauraceae (avocado and cinnamon family).

RANGE NE India, Thailand, to Malay Peninsula, Singapore, Borneo, Sumatra, Java and Palawan.

Temburong (HP)

Striped Bluebottle ■ *Graphium bathycles* (Zinken, 1831)
(Borneo race – *bathycloides*) [Striped Jay]

HABITAT Lowland to hills, forest, along rivers.   **ABUNDANCE** Locally common.

Temburong (CP)

DESCRIPTION Sexes similar. Two thin, black parallel horizontal stripes on a pale blue background are the dominant feature when settled with wings back. Noticeable flush of yellow upwards from base of hindwing, and row of five orange-red submarginal spots in dark border. The vibrancy of the colours varies depending on the angle of the light. Pattern above similar but stronger blue with no yellow or red.

SIMILAR SPECIES One of seven very similar species distinguished by parallel black stripes and significant yellow flush on hindwing underside.

HABITAT AND HABITS Seen along rivers or streams in forested areas. Males come to damp ground to take up moisture enriched with minerals and often remain settled, puddling, for a protracted period. Congregates with others of the same species or diverse species. Regularly seen with the very similar Blue Jay G. *evemon*. Active in full sun throughout the day. Fast, agile flight. Female rarely seen.

LARVAL FOOD PLANT Magnoliaceae (magnolia family).

RANGE Malay Peninsula, Borneo, Sumatra, Java and Palawan. Note that the similar, but now recognized as distinct G. *chironides* flies in NE India, S China to Malay Peninsula.

Tailed Jay ■ *Graphium agamemnon* (Linnaeus, 1758)

(Race – *agamemnon*) [Tailed Green Jay, Green Spotted Triangle]

HABITAT Forested areas, along rivers, larger islands.   **ABUNDANCE** Locally common.

DESCRIPTION Sexes similar. Upperside strikingly patterned all over with bright green spots on a black background. Underside has similar pattern but less extensive green on a bronzy-brown background and some buffy-pink markings. Short tail to hindwing that is slightly longer and more obvious in female than in male.

HABITAT AND HABITS Found from the lowlands to the hills, at forest edge and along riverbanks. Also on larger islands. Active under the midday sun. Usually seen singly but joins other species in puddle groups. Arrives abruptly, flies in fast and, closing its wings, settles rapidly. Prolonged puddler but restless, shifting position frequently. Visits flowers for nectar. Note that throughout much of the rest of its range it is recorded in open country, villages, parks and gardens. 'Extensive planting of its larval food plants like mast tree … and custard apple has brought this forest-dweller into urban areas' (Isaac Kehimkar, *The Book of Indian Butterflies*, 2008).

LARVAL FOOD PLANT Lauraceae (cinnamon and avocado family), Annonaceae (sweetsop and soursop family), Magnoliaceae (magnolia family) *Michelia* spp.

RANGE India and Sri Lanka, east through S China to Taiwan, south through the Philippines, Malay Peninsula, Singapore, Sumatra, Java, Borneo, Palawan, east to New Guinea, Solomon Islands and south to NE Australia.

Temburong (CP)

Five-bar Swordtail ■ *Graphium antiphates* (Cramer, 1775)
(Borneo race – *itamputi*)

HABITAT Lowland to hill forest, along rivers.   **ABUNDANCE** Not uncommon, local.

DESCRIPTION Sexes similar. Underside has conspicuous black bars on forewing, lime green on basal half of both wings and buffy-orange on outer half of hindwing. Long, straight, pointed tail on each hindwing gives rise to the common name. Entirely white above except for black bars on forewing, black edging to hindwing and dark tails. (Two further subspecies occur on Banggi and Balambangan islands).

SIMILAR SPECIES The most common of five species of swordtail that occur in Borneo. If underwing is showing, distinguished by green and extensive orange colouring. If only overwing is visible, distinguished by number of black bars and lack of red dots. With white above and swift flight, can be confused with *Appias* of the Pieridae family (p. 53).

HABITAT AND HABITS Flies very swiftly along forest streams or tracks at 2–5m height, landing abruptly. Males come to damp, sandy riverbanks or gravelled paths for moisture. Usually seen as a singleton but will join other species, including other *Graphium* spp. in puddling groups. Prefers sun and sometimes basks on low foliage. Attracted to flowers for nectar.

LARVAL FOOD PLANT Lauraceae (cinnamon, belian family), Annonaceae (sweetsop, soursop family), on *Desmos lawii*, Malay Peninsula.

RANGE India, Sri Lanka east to SE China, Hong Kong, south to Malay Peninsula, Singapore, Borneo, Palawan, Sumatra, Java and east to Alor.

Temburong (HP)

White Dragontail ■ *Lamproptera curius* (Fabricius, 1787)
(Borneo race – *curius*)

HABITAT By rivers within forest. **ABUNDANCE** Uncommon.

Temburong (HP)

DESCRIPTION Sexes similar. Members of the *Lamproptera genus* have a unique and unmistakable shape. Small, with exceptionally long tails to hindwing, described by entomologist Thomas Enriquez as 'a long, frail streamer' and in flight looking like 'a string of pearls'. Predominantly dark brown with a broad white stripe running down centre of both forewing and hindwing. Forewing has black border and triangular transparent panel.

SIMILAR SPECIES Very similar to the Green Dragontail (p. 46), which occurs in similar habitat. Distinguished by having pale band on wings, white not tinged greenish, and comparatively smaller transparent panel in forewing.

HABITAT AND HABITS Found in lowland to hills by sunlit streams in forest. Flight low and swift. Males come to damp ground along river's edge or on forest pathways to puddle, sometimes joining other species in a group. Often rubs its long tails together in a shimmering motion on landing. Frequently expels surplus water. Generally occurs singly, but also reported in small flocks. Female visits flowers for nectar.

LARVAL FOOD PLANT Hernandiaceae, on *Illigera pulchra* in Borneo.

RANGE NE India, east to S China, Hong Kong, and south through Malay Peninsula to Sumatra, Java, Borneo and Palawan.

Green Dragontail ■ *Lamproptera meges* (Zinken, 1831)
(Borneo race – *meges*)

HABITAT Lowland to hill forest, along streams.   **ABUNDANCE** Not common.

Mulu (CP)

DESCRIPTION Sexes similar. Small with relatively short, stubby forewings and elongated hindwings with disproportionately long, broad, white-tipped tails twisted at ends. Tails usually held rigid behind. A pale greenish-white band runs across forewing and hindwing, and gives the species its common name. Forewing has a large, transparent panel taking up approximately two-thirds of the wing's surface.

SIMILAR SPECIES Distinguished from the very similar but less common White Dragontail (p. 45), which occurs in similar habitat, by greenish tinge to pale band on wings and larger transparent panel on forewing.

HABITAT AND HABITS Occurs in forested areas from the lowlands to the hills. Usually seen as a singleton along sunlit streams, where it comes to take up water, alighting among pebbles in the shallows. Flies low and swiftly, sometimes almost hovering at one spot, then darting quickly forwards. Due to this flight pattern, coupled with its size and long, rigid tails, it can easily be mistaken for a dragonfly at first sight.

LARVAL FOOD PLANT Hernandiaceae, *Illigera* spp.

RANGE NE India to S China and south through Malay Peninsula, Sumatra, Java, Borneo, Palawan, the Philippines to Sulawesi.

Bornean Jezebel ■ *Delias eumolpe* (Grose-Smith, 1889) ⓔ

HABITAT Hill to montane forest.   **ABUNDANCE** Not uncommon

DESCRIPTION Sexes dissimilar. Male under hindwing predominantly yellow with a red patch at the 'shoulder', and a row of six large red spots set in a broad black border. Under forewing black with a row of four yellow spots at the apex. Male above all white except for dark forewing-tips. Female underside as male, but dark dusted across hindwing. Female upperside mostly black, except white at base of hindwing.

> **MISTLETOE**
> Mistletoe (Loranthaceae) is the favoured larval food plant of the *Delias* butterflies. Mistletoes are shrubby, leafy parasitic plants with showy flowers, whose seeds are dispersed by birds and which grow on the upper branches of the host tree.

SIMILAR SPECIES The Sulu Jezebel (p. 48) and *D. pasithoe* both have similar colouring, but lack the distinctive submarginal red spots and have more slender forewings.

HABITAT AND HABITS A butterfly of forested areas from hills to high mountains. Often found along ridges. Generally keeps to the canopy, but occasionally comes down low by streams or at the forest edge, where it can be more easily seen. It has a slow, fluttery flight, seldom settling. Tolerates typical montane weather and flies even in cool and cloudy conditions.

LARVAL FOOD PLANT Not recorded, but most likely Loranthaceae (mistletoe family).

RANGE Endemic to Borneo.

Mesilau River, 1,200m (CP)

Sulu Jezebel ■ *Delias henningia* (Eschscholtz, 1821)
(Borneo race – *pandemia*)

HABITAT Hill to lower montane forest.   **ABUNDANCE** Not uncommon.

DESCRIPTION Sexes similar. Predominantly charcoal-black. Under hindwing brightly coloured, with red at base and large yellow panel traversed by heavy black veins. Forewing underside black with diffuse white band and arc of white spots towards apex. Upperside mainly black with no red, much reduced yellow area and no pale band on forewing. Two grey spots near base of hindwing, absent in female.

SIMILAR SPECIES The Bornean Jezebel (p. 47) has a distinctive row of red submarginal spots on hindwing underside. *D. pasithoe* has more extensive yellow on under hindwing. *D. ninus* has more red and paler yellow on under hindwing. Above has red at base of hindwing and yellow patch replaced by white.

HABITAT AND HABITS Butterfly of forested areas on hills and lower elevations on mountains. Usually seen at the forest edge, where it comes down to take nectar from flowering bushes or wayside flowers. Not easily disturbed when feeding. Species of the genus *Delias* are distasteful to birds and have aposematic colouring with reds and yellows that act to warn off predators (p. 20).

LARVAL FOOD PLANT Loranthaceae (mistletoe family).

RANGE N Borneo, Palawan and the Philippines.

Kokol Ridge (CP)

Painted Jezebel ■ *Delias hyparete* (Linnaeus, 1758)
(Borneo race – *diva*)

HABITAT Lowland to hills, forest to village.   **ABUNDANCE** Uncommon.

Mulu (HP)

DESCRIPTION Sexes dissimilar. Underside alike. Hindwing has bright red submarginal border and yellow spreading outwards from wing-base. White ground colour with veins and wing margins heavily blackened. Male above all white, with only forewing veins and apical area darkened, whereas female above is much more heavily dark dusted across wings. Slender forewing and rounded hindwing typical of *Delias* species.

HABITAT AND HABITS Found from the lowlands to the hills, and from forest to village edge, but most common in lowland secondary vegetation. Flies among the treetops where its larval food plant, mistletoe, grows. Descends occasionally to drink nectar from flowers in sunny clearings. Photo shows male nectaring on a *Nauclea* tree at the river's edge. The red, yellow and black warning colours protect it from potential predators (p. 20). Active throughout the day and sometimes even at dusk.

LARVAL FOOD PLANT Loranthaceae (mistletoe family) in Borneo. Elsewhere reported on a wide variety of plants across 10 families, including Coconut Palm (*Cocos nucifera*, Palmae) and Cocoa (*Theobroma cacao*, Sterculiaceae) in Malay Peninsula, and Mango (*Mangifera indica*, Anacardiaceae) in Thailand.

RANGE E and NE India, east through S China to Taiwan, Hong Kong, south through the Philippines, Southeast Asia, Malay Peninsula, Singapore, Sumatra, Java, Borneo to Bali.

Psyche - *Leptosia nina* (Fabricius, 1793)
(Borneo race – *malayana*)

HABITAT Lowland to hills, edge of forest.   **ABUNDANCE** Locally common.

Poring (HP)

DESCRIPTION Sexes similar. All white. Forewing above has single, central, large black spot and black tip. On underside forewing is marked as above, but hindwing is white, faintly streaked with fine greenish lines. A small, delicate butterfly with rounded, elongated wings. Orange-tipped antennae. Restless and seldom settles.

HABITAT AND HABITS Usually seen at the forest margin or in forest clearings. It partly flutters and partly floats very low over wayside vegetation, like a fragment of tissue paper carried on a warm breeze. Although it appears weak it flies almost incessantly throughout the day, rarely stopping to rest or feed. Comes to flowers for nectar.

LARVAL FOOD PLANT Capparaceae (caper family), *Cleome rutidosperma*; on *Capparis heyneana* and *Crataeva religiosa* in Malay Peninsula.

RANGE India, Sri Lanka east through Myanmar, S China, Hong Kong (rare), Taiwan, the Philippines, Palawan and south through Thailand, Malay Peninsula, Singapore, Borneo, Sulawesi, Sumatra, Java, east to Timor, Tanimbar and south to NW Australia (the Kimberley).

> *Psyche* is from the Greek, meaning breath, life or soul.

Orange Gull ■ *Cepora iudith* (Fabricius, 1787)
(Borneo race – *hespera*)

HABITAT Lowland to hill forest, larger islands.   **ABUNDANCE** Locally common.

DESCRIPTION Sexes differ. Male under hindwing yellow with brown border and darkened veins, as shown. Under forewing white with broad brown border flecked with white. White above with inwardly serrated black border and conspicuous large, yellow-orange patch at tip of hindwing, which is distinctive. Female has rounder wings and similar pattern, but altogether darker with heavier border, more heavily dark-dusted veins and only a faint orange patch above. Variable.

Illustration of ♂ overwing showing distinctive orange patches

SIMILAR SPECIES The Chocolate Albatross (p. 53), of similar habits and habitat, has broader brown border without flecking and more elongated forewing.

HABITAT AND HABITS Found in lowland forest, frequenting sunlit sites. Males take up fluids from sandy riverbanks. Usually occurs singly, but also readily congregates with others of the same or different species. Very restless when puddling, typically taking flight and re-alighting every 20 seconds or so, even while surrounding butterflies remain static. This habit enables a glimpse of the distinctive upperside orange patch. Flight low and strong.

LARVAL FOOD PLANT Capparaceae (caper family)); recorded on *Capparis* in Java.

RANGE S Myanmar, S Thailand, Malay Peninsula, Sumatra, Java and Borneo. Recorded on Maratua Island, off Kalimantan.

Temburong (CP)

Bornean Gull ■ *Cepora pactolicus* (Butler, 1865) ⓔ

HABITAT Lowland to lower montane forest.   **ABUNDANCE** Not common.

DESCRIPTION Sexes differ. Male under hindwing, as shown, yellow with broad black border with uniform row of large white flecks and all veins heavily blackened. Under forewing all white with apex broadly darkened but streaked with white. Male above all white except heavily darkened forewing apex and partial black inwardly serrated border to hindwing. Female underwing similar to male, but over-wing darker than male's with broadly darkened veins and broad, hazy dark border to hindwing.

SIMILAR SPECIES Differs from the Orange Gull (p. 51) by lack of orange patch on upperside and having prominent white flecks in under hindwing border. Also similar to Smokey Albatross (p.56).

HABITAT AND HABITS Inhabits forested areas. Seen along riverbanks in lowland forest. Males take moisture from wet ground and will join a puddling group with other species including the Orange Gull, which usually outnumbers it by approximately 5:1. Recorded near Mount Kinabalu Park HQ at around 1,500m; also that it was widely distributed throughout Sarawak and had been found in different forest types, from lowland to limestone forests.

LARVAL FOOD PLANT Not recorded – but most likely feeds on Capparaceae (Caper family), as do all other species of *Cepora* whose food plant is so far recorded.

RANGE Endemic to Borneo.

Temburong (HP)

Chocolate Albatross ■ *Appias lyncida* (Cramer, 1777)
(Borneo race – *enarete*)

HABITAT Lowland to hill forest, by rivers.   **ABUNDANCE** Locally common.

Temburong (CP)

DESCRIPTION Sexes differ. Male underside has hindwing sulphur-yellow with a very broad, chocolate-brown border that gives rise to the English common name. Male above all white with a narrow, toothed black margin to both wings. Female white, with veins and outer expanse of wings heavily dusted with dark brown and underneath hindwing faintly yellow. Note that in the Borneo race the male has a much broader chocolate border, and is approx. 25 per cent larger than other races.

SIMILAR SPECIES The Orange Gull *Cepora iudith* (p.51), of similar habits and habitat, has a narrower under-hindwing brown border, flecked with yellow, a less angular forewing and is smaller.

HABITAT AND HABITS Inhabits forests from the lowlands to the hills. A robust flyer. Male is active in strong sunshine. Most likely to be seen taking water at damp patches along banks of streams or rivers, frequently in the company of other butterflies. The contrasting yellow and brown are aposematic (warning) colours (p. 20). The rarely seen female frequents the forest undergrowth but visits flowers for nectar.

LARVAL FOOD PLANT Capparaceae (caper family); recorded on *Crateva religiosa* and *Capparis micracantha* in Malay Peninsula and elsewhere.

RANGE India, Sri Lanka, east to S China, Hong Kong (rare), Taiwan, south to the Philippines, Palawan, Malay Peninsula, Singapore, Borneo, Sulawesi, Sumatra, Java and east to Timor.

Striped Albatross ■ *Appias libythea* (Fabricius, 1775)
(Borneo race – *olferna*)

HABITAT Lowlands, scrub, open spaces.   **ABUNDANCE** Locally common.

WINGSPAN 50–60mm

♂ *Sg. Wain (HP)*   ♀ *Panaga, Brunei (HP)*

DESCRIPTION Sexes differ. The male, in flight, gives the impression of being pure white, and is all white above except for a thin, scalloped black border. Once settled with wings back, the prominent black-dusted veins create the distinctive striped appearance that gives rise to the common name. The female has more subdued colouring with extensive grey-brown dusting along the veins and wing margins causing a 'dappled-shade effect'. The under hindwing is grey-yellow in part. More rounded wings that in male. Both sexes have a yellow basal streak on the hindwing underside.

SIMILAR SPECIES Other *Appias*, in flight, but smaller than the other species.

HABITAT AND HABITS Male flies very fast in clearings in secondary growth and scrub, in full sunshine, at moderate height of 1–4m. Easier to see when taking moisture from damp ground, sometimes in the company of others. Female is more elusive but can be seen nectaring on wayside flowers. Elsewhere reported in roadsides, suburban areas and gardens. Migratory in India.

LARVAL FOOD PLANT No Borneo records. Capparaceae (caper family) in Malay Peninsula, Singapore and India.

RANGE From India and Sri Lanka, through Nepal, Bhutan, Myanmar, Malay Peninsula and Singapore, to Borneo, the Philippines and south to Christmas Island (Australia). Not previously recorded in Borneo; above photographs are thought to be the first published photos from Borneo.

Orange Albatross ■ *Appias nero* (Fabricius, 1793)
(Borneo race – *chelidon*)

HABITAT By streams in forest.   **ABUNDANCE** Not uncommon.

DESCRIPTION Sexes differ. Male unmistakable. Entirely bright reddish-orange above with no markings other than darkened veins and forewing-tip. Underside entirely yellow-orange. Female orange above with broad, diffuse black border and darkened wing-bases. Under forewing as overwing and under hindwing pale grey with broad, diffuse dark grey border. As in all *Appias*, forewing is noticeably pointed and hindwing is rounded.

HABITAT AND HABITS Occurs in lowland to hills. Flies in sunny places within forested areas. Flight very fast. Male typically encountered settled on a sandy riverbank or gravelled road surface taking up water. Occurs as a singleton or sometimes in a mixed-species puddling group usually dominated by other pierids. Female generally flies in the canopy and is rarely seen.

LARVAL FOOD PLANT Capparaceae (caper family), Euphorbiaceae (tapioca, rubber and spurge family); on *Capparis micracantha*, *Drypetes macrophylla* and *D. longifolia* (Putranjivaceae) in the Philippines. Note that the leaves of Capparaceae contain glucosinolates and those of certain Euphorbiaceae and Putranjivaceae contain white, milky latex, both of which make the larvae that feed on them and subsequently the adult butterflies toxic to predators (p. 20).

RANGE N India, Myanmar, Thailand, Malay Peninsula, Borneo, Sumatra, Java, the Philippines, Sulawesi and Buru.

Tabin (CP)

Smokey Albatross ■ *Appias cardena* (Hewitson, 1861)
(Borneo race – *cardena*)

HABITAT Lowland to mountains, forest edge.   **ABUNDANCE** Uncommon.

DESCRIPTION Sexes differ. Male under-hindwing predominantly yellow, shading to milky-white with darkened veins and a broad diffuse smokey-grey border of uneven width. Under-forewing white with pale-streaked dark apex. White above, with black border to wings broader at forewing apex and inwardly toothed. Female similar underneath with stronger yellow. Similar above to male, but has wider black border to both wings.

SIMILAR SPECIES In flight many of the albatrosses (*Appias* genus), which are white with black edging, especially the Chocolate Albatross (p. 53). When settled with hindwing underside showing looks most similar to the Bornean Gull (p. 52), *Delias singhapura* and *D. baracasa*, but all have pale flecks in a dark border of uniform width and yellow evenly spread across entire hindwing.

HABITAT AND HABITS Occurs in forested areas at all elevations from lowland to mountains, up to 2,000m. Found at the forest edge in the open and on forest paths. Males come to damp, sandy soil to take moisture. Usually occurs singly.

LARVAL FOOD PLANT No records. Quite likely on Capparaceae or Euphorbiaceae, like most other *Appias*.

RANGE Malay Peninsula, Sumatra and Borneo.

WINGSPAN 65–70mm

Mt Alab (HP)

Triangle White ■ *Saletara panda* (Butler, 1898)
(Borneo race – *distanti*) [Malaysian Albatross]

HABITAT Lowland to hill forest, by streams.   **ABUNDANCE** Locally common.

DESCRIPTION Sexes differ. Male above creamy-white with a uniformly narrow but well-defined black border to forewing. Underneath entirely rich yellow with no markings. Female above white with a thick dark border to both wings, heavier on forewing, which is also dark dusted at base. Hindwing flushed with pale yellow. An elegant butterfly with an acutely pointed forewing, closely related to the *Appias*.

SIMILAR SPECIES The White Albatross *Appias albina*, is very similar, but male is entirely white both under and over, and lacks the distinctive narrow black border to forewing. Female has a less well defined and patchy dark border.

Distinctive, sharply triangular forewings, Temburong (HP)

HABITAT AND HABITS Occurs in forested areas. Rarely found above 650m. Male takes moisture from sandy soil on riverbanks, or along forest paths in the sunshine. Frequently seen in the company of other pierids. Occasionally seen basking on low vegetation. Invariably settles with wings back, forming a unique and distinctive triangle shape. Female generally keeps to the forest and is rarely seen.

LARVAL FOOD PLANT Capparaceae (caper family).

RANGE Nicobar Islands east through Malay Peninsula, Borneo, the Philippines, Sumatra, Java, Bali, and larger islands throughout the archipelago to New Guinea.

Temburong (CP)

Great Orange Tip ■ *Hebomoia glaucippe* (Linnaeus, 1758)
(Borneo race – *borneensis*)

HABITAT By streams within forest.   **ABUNDANCE** Locally common.

DESCRIPTION Sexes differ. This is the largest of the
Pieridae family in the Oriental region and one of the largest
pierids in the world. Male striking, with upperside white and
bold orange triangular patch bordered in black at forewing-
tip. In female, orange is either absent or very indistinct. She
also has a heavy, black-serrated margin on the hindwing and
inner to that a row of large black spots. Female less often
seen than male. In both sexes, underside finely striated

Illustration of ♂ upperside

sandy-beige with darker veins, and resembles a dead leaf.

HABITAT AND HABITS Occurs from the lowlands up into the hills. Found by streams or
rivers in forested areas. Male has a strong but erratic flight and flies in the open under the
direct sun. Usually flies high but comes down for nectar or to damp ground for water. Will
often join a group of other species mud puddling on the shore of a river, but in contrast
to the other species does not stay long before flying off along the river course. May return
later but is always restless.

LARVAL FOOD PLANT Capparaceae (caper family), including *Crateva religiosa* and the
climber *Capparis moonii*. See opposite.

RANGE India, Sri Lanka, east to S China, Hong Kong, Taiwan and Ryukyu Islands,
south to the Philippines, Sulawesi, Halmahera, south through Vietnam, Laos, Cambodia,
Thailand, Malay Peninsula, Borneo, Sumatra, Java, and east to Tanimbar.

Temburong (CP)

CAMOUFLAGE, CHEMICALS & WARNING COLOURS

The Great Orange Tip is a good example of both 'warning colours' and 'camouflage' colouring. The bright orange wing-tips of the male are very conspicuous in flight, but on landing it closes its wings instantaneously so that only the camouflaged underside is visible. It passes for a dead leaf among vegetation or on a leaf-strewn sandy river bank, where it blends instantly into the background and is barely discernible from just a few feet away even if you have just watched it settle.

An Orange Tip ♀, with black border to white wings, nectaring on an Ixora flower, Poring (CP)

The larvae of the Great Orange Tip feed on plants in the Capparaceae (caper family). Related to Brassicaceae (cabbage family) and Cleomaceae, these plants contain mustard oils or glucosinolates, chemicals that the larvae sequester, making both the larvae and subsequently the adult butterfly unpalatable to potential predators. The black and white markings of the over wing, reinforced with bright orange in the male, are warning colours, signalling this unpalatability to predators to deter possible attack.

In Borneo the Great Orange Tip is a forest dweller whose larvae feed on wild plants of the Capparaceae, particularly the *Crateva* genus, which are mostly found growing near water, for example along riverbanks. However, in Hong Kong and Vietnam the Great Orange Tip is reported to occur more widely and even in urban areas (Bascombe, Monastyrskii), where its larvae feed on cultivated plants of the Capparaceae. In Hong Kong the larvae feed on *Crateva religiosa*, a deciduous tree

that many years ago was planted along roadsides. More widely, *C. religiosa* is often planted near temples and it is a larval food plant across the region, including in India, Thailand, China, the Philippines and the Malay Peninsula.

Crateva religiosa, *Singapore Botanic Gardens (HP)*

Squared Yellow ■ *Dercas gobrias* (Hewitson, 1864)
(Borneo race – *gobrias*) [Notched Yellow]

HABITAT Forest, along rivers.   **ABUNDANCE** Not uncommon.

DESCRIPTION Sexes differ. Male sulphur-yellow, female creamy-white. Distinctive features are squared off shape of wings, squarish, dark brown patch at forewing apex, serrated wing edges, and hindwing angled to a point. Underneath, there is a faint brown streak crossing both wings and a small, irregular brown mark mid-forewing. The orange-tipped antennae are disproportionately short.

SIMILAR SPECIES Bigger than all the other yellow butterflies, such as the *Eurema* species (pp. 65–67) and Tree Yellow (p. 68), with a squarish outline instead of rounded wings.

HABITAT AND HABITS Found in primary forest from the lowlands to the hills, generally along streams or rivers. Flies fast in sunlit areas. Usually seen singly. Males come to damp ground or the river's edge for mineral-enriched water, where once settled they often stay for

Temburong (HP)

some considerable time while other puddling species come and go. Typically, rests hanging upside down under a large leaf, where it blends in remarkably.

LARVAL FOOD PLANT Not known but an unidentified vine in the Leguminosae (pea family), *Dalbergia* genus, has been reported from Borneo.

RANGE Malay Peninsula, Borneo, Sumatra and Java.

THE GREEN REFLEX

This species is a good example of the 'green reflex'. As entomologist and taxonomist Dick Vane-Wright (2003) writes of a similarly coloured pierid butterfly:

> Viewed in isolation from leaves, their undersides seem to have no more than a passing resemblance to leaves. Being pale lemon yellow rather than green they seem to be the wrong colour. However, as discussed by the Russian entomologist E. N. Schwanwitsch, they exhibit a poorly understood phenomenon that he called the 'green reflex'. When sitting among foliage, the wing undersides reflect or take on the green colour of the leaves surrounding them and then the butterflies become very difficult to see – another wonderful example of camouflage.

Photographed with flash, the true yellow colour of the butterfly makes it stand out. Photographed using only natural light, the butterfly reflects the green colour of the leaf and blends in.

Hidden in plain sight – a Squared Yellow has just settled on the underside of a large leaf, and both in terms of shape and colour instantaneously blends in with its natural surroundings. The camouflage is helped by the settling posture involving hanging under the leaf. Kokol Ridge, ridgetop path (HP)

Wanderer ■ *Pareronia valeria* (Cramer, 1776)
(Borneo race – *lutescens*)

HABITAT Lowland to hills, edge of forest.

ABUNDANCE Not uncommon.

♂ *overwing, Danum (HP)*

DESCRIPTION Sexes differ greatly. Male has predominantly pale blue wings with prominent black veins and black border. Underside paler with no border. Female has much more extensive black markings and the interveinal spaces are greyish-white except for a flush of yellow on the hindwings. Female variable with some individuals duller than others.
SIMILAR SPECIES Female mimics the Yellow Glassy Tiger (p. 71), and generally resembles members of the *Parantica*, *Tirumala* and *Ideopsis* genera – the tigers (Nymphalidae) (pp. 69–74); for mimicry, see p. 22).
HABITAT AND HABITS
Occurs along the forest edge in the lowlands and hills, favouring open, sunny places. Flies throughout the heat of the day. Male flies strongly and very fast, and is often seen at a height of about 2m. Female flies more slowly and is less often sighted. Both sexes visit flowers for nectar. Males come to wet ground to drink. Usually seen singly.

LARVAL FOOD PLANT
Capparaceae (caper family); on *Capparis heydeana* in Malay Peninsula; on *C. zeylanica*, *C. micracantha* and *C. sepiaria* in Palawan.
RANGE India, Myanmar, Thailand, Malay Peninsula, Palawan, the Philippines, Borneo, Sumatra, Java and east to Timor.

♂ *underwing, Mulu (HP)*

Mottled Emigrant ■ *Catopsilia pyranthe* (Linnaeus, 1758)
(Borneo race – *pyranthe*)

HABITAT Lowlands, open secondary growth.   **ABUNDANCE** Moderately common.

DESCRIPTION Sexes similar. Medium sized. Underneath a pale greenish-yellow, faintly mottled all over with fine brown streaks. Above all white with a black border to the forewing apex, wider in female than in male. A sometimes faint, black dot on mid-forewing. Less common than the Lemon Emigrant (p. 64) in Borneo. Occurs as a single race throughout its range, but in Australia a pale form also occurs.

HABITAT AND HABITS Found in the lowlands from the shore inland. Frequents open, sunny spaces, such as grassy clearings with scattered bushes, from villages to forest edge. Active throughout the heat of the day, flying rapidly at low level. Settles to feed or rest with wings back. Both sexes visit flowers and males are sometimes seen at damp ground. See also p. 14, larva. Migratory. Mass migrations recorded in India and Australia, but in lesser numbers and over smaller distances than for the Lemon Emigrant.

LARVAL FOOD PLANT Leguminosae (pea family) *Cassia* and *Senna* genera, especially *Senna alata*, 'Seven Golden Candlesticks'. See also p. 168, food plants.

RANGE India, east to S China, Taiwan, the Ryukyu Islands (Japan), south through the Philippines, Southeast Asia, Malay Peninsula, Singapore, Borneo, Sumatra, Java east to Vanuatu (but absent from Timor and New Guinea), and south to N and E Australia.

Mulu (HP)

Lemon Emigrant ■ *Catopsilia pomona* (Fabricius, 1775)

(Borneo race – *pomona*) [Common Emigrant]

HABITAT Lowland to hills, sunny, flower-rich sites.   **ABUNDANCE** Common

♀ *of Pomona group, Poring*   ♂ *of Crocale group, Tabin*

DESCRIPTION Sexes differ. Seven different forms are recognized but intermediates also occur. There are two different 'groups', previously believed to be two different species. Members of the '*Pomona*' group have at least a little red pigment. In the male, seen with red-ringed silvery-white spots on the under hindwing. Ground colour pale greenish-yellow. In the female there is a slightly orange tint on the underside, which may be further marked or extensively blotched with dull red. Associated with the dry season. Migratory, often seen in their thousands. '*Crocale*' group members have no red or orange pigment. The underside is unmarked, without spots, and both male and female are entirely pale lemon-yellow below. Associated with the wet season. Non-migratory.

In both groups, male is white above with an irregular splash of yellow at the wing-bases and the thinnest of black margins at the forewing apex. Females are milky-white to lemon-yellow above with dark borders of varying widths. In most of its range, butterflies of the unmarked '*Crocale*' group are considered more common.

HABITAT AND HABITS Mainly found in the lowlands but also into the hills; in open, sunny places. Active through the heat of the day. Both sexes spend much of their time at

nectar flowers. Males also come to damp patches along muddy paths or gravel roads, often singly, but sometimes in large congregations. Swift in flight.

LARVAL FOOD PLANT Leguminosae (pea family), particularly *Cassia fistula*, *Senna siamea* and *Butea monosperma* in Malay Peninsula.

RANGE India, east through S China, to Taiwan and the Ryukyu Islands (Japan), south to the Philippines, Malay Peninsula, Singapore, Borneo, and east to New Guinea and Vanuatu, south to N Australia.

Illustration of ♂ overwing

Common Grass Yellow ■ *Eurema hecabe* (Linnaeus, 1758)
(Borneo race – *hecabe*)

HABITAT All elevations, most habitats. **ABUNDANCE** Very common.

DESCRIPTION Sexes similar. Small, bright yellow butterfly with a strong dark border to both wings above. Female slightly paler than male, with hindwing border inwardly diffuse. Underside has a scattering of small, rust-brown markings. Very variable.
SIMILAR SPECIES The most common of 10 similar species, most of which are indistinguishable in the field.
HABITAT AND HABITS Found at all elevations and in most habitats, from seashore to gardens, waste ground, roadside verges, farmland, lowland primary forest, along rivers and in hill to montane forest. Restless. Flutters low over grass or among bushes in sunny locations. Active throughout the day, frequently stopping to take nectar at wild flowers. Settles with wings closed. Males sometimes congregate at damp ground.
LARVAL FOOD PLANT Feeds predominantly on Leguminosae, Fabaceae (pea family), including *Acacia*, *Albizia* and *Senna*, but on a great variety from 14 plant families.
RANGE Widely distributed from tropical Africa, the Middle East, India, Sri Lanka, east to S China, S Japan, south through the Philippines, Southeast Asia to Malay Peninsula, Singapore, Borneo, Sumatra, Java, east to New Guinea, Fiji, Tonga, and south to N and E Australia.

Tg. Aru (CP)

Chocolate Grass Yellow ■ *Eurema sari* (Horsfield, 1829)
(Borneo race – *sodalis*)

HABITAT Forest, lowland to highlands. **ABUNDANCE** Not uncommon.

DESCRIPTION Sexes similar, with female paler than male. Small yellow butterfly. Underside has a conspicuous and distinctive squarish dark brown patch at forewing-tip. Also, a scattering of small, rust-brown marks. Upperside has a clearly defined black border to both wings. Border is broader and inwardly irregular on forewing, and paler and more diffuse in female than in male.

SIMILAR SPECIES One of 10 butterflies in the *Eurema* genus in Borneo that are virtually indistinguishable in flight. If settled with underwing showing, the brown apical patch is distinctive. Only the less common *E. simulatrix* has a similar brown patch, although this is less well defined and mottled through with yellow.

HABITAT AND HABITS Inhabits inland lowland, hill or highland forest, usually near streams or rivers. Prefers open forest but generally remains in shade or semi-shade. Flight low, slow, fluttering and erratic. Visits flowers and damp ground. Attracted to human sweat.

LARVAL FOOD PLANT Leguminosae (Caesalpinioideae) (pea and mimosa family). Reported on *Senna siamea* in Malay Peninsula.

RANGE NE India, Sri Lanka, Myanmar, Thailand, east to Vietnam, south to Malay Peninsula, Singapore, Sumatra, Java, Borneo and Palawan.

Sungai Wain (HP)

Banded Grass Yellow ■ *Eurema nicevillei* (Butler, 1898)
(Borneo race – *nicevillei*) [Malayan Grass Yellow]

HABITAT Forest, lowland to hills, and larger islands. **ABUNDANCE** Moderately common.

Mulu (CP)

DESCRIPTION Sexes similar. Small yellow butterfly with neat dark borders to wings above. Borders wider in female than in male, especially on hindwing. On underside there is a row of five faint but discernible brown marks in an arc on each wing. Also a scattering of a further few faint, rusty-brown marks across both wings.

SIMILAR SPECIES The most common of only three *Eurema* butterflies, in which the forewing black border is continued along the rear wing edge (the dorsum). This forms a distinctive horizontal band visible in flight. Distinguished from *E. tominia* by habitat, *E. tominia* being montane. *E. alitha* is relatively rare. Note that the similar *E. tilaha* is found in neighbouring Java and Bali.

HABITAT AND HABITS Found in relatively open parts of the forest such as along paths, at the edge of clearings or beside rivers. Flies in shade or sun, keeping low. Visits flowers for nectar. Males settle to take up mineral-rich water, sometimes joining puddle groups with other species, including other grass yellows. Settles with wings closed.

LARVAL FOOD PLANT Leguminosae (pea family); recorded on *Senna siamea* in Thailand.

RANGE S Thailand, Langkawi, Malay Peninsula, Tioman, Sumatra, Nias and Mentawai Islands, to Borneo.

Tree Yellow ■ *Gandaca harina* (Horsfield, 1829)
(Borneo race – *elis*)

HABITAT Lowlands to hills, forest, forest edge.   **ABUNDANCE** Moderately common.

Kimanis (HP)

DESCRIPTION Sexes similar. Entirely pale lemon-yellow with a greenish tinge. Underside has no markings in either sex. Male above has narrow black border at forewing apex tapering along outer wing margin. Female above paler, with a slightly broader border toothed at one point. Hindwing well rounded.

SIMILAR SPECIES Closely resembles species of the *Eurema* genus (pp. 65–67) but is paler. Distinguished by complete lack of spots or markings on underside.

HABITAT AND HABITS Found in primary forest and adjacent secondary growth from the lowlands to the hills. Prefers shade or semi-shade. Sips water from damp, sandy ground along forest paths or stream edge, sometimes alone but more often in the company of other pierids. Comes to flowers for nectar. Male more often seen than female.

LARVAL FOOD PLANT Rhamnaceae (buckthorn, jujube family); the larva feeds and sometimes pupates inside the rolled leaves of the food plant *Ventilago oblongifolia*; Connaraceae (zebra wood family).

RANGE NE India (Sikkim), Myanmar, Thailand, east to the Philippines, Palawan, south to the Malay Peninsula, Singapore, Borneo, Sumatra and Java, and east to Sumba.

Common Tiger ■ *Danaus genutia* (Cramer, 1779)
(Borneo race – *intensa*) [Orange Tiger]

HABITAT Open country, lowland to hills.   **ABUNDANCE** Locally common.

Poring (CP)

DESCRIPTION Sexes similar. The most aptly named of all the tiger butterflies, with bold black lines on a strongly tawny-orange background. Broadly black apex inner to which is an irregular transverse band of large white spots. Double row of small white dots within black border along wing margin. Underside paler, especially hindwing. Males have a pouch containing scent scales on hindwing, visible at close proximity. Note that in the Malay Peninsula, two forms occur – one with white hindwings, the other with orange.

HABITAT AND HABITS Found in the lowlands to the hills, especially near streams. Frequents open, sunny places with secondary growth such as weed-strewn verges of quiet rural tracks, cultivated areas and disturbed habitats from forest clearings to wasteland, but typically near forest. Comes to flowers for nectar. Robust, with a strong, slow flight.

LARVAL FOOD PLANT Asclepiadaceae (milkweed family), particularly on *Cynanchum* spp. – more than 25 host plants recorded for the region, including *Asclepias curassavica* (p. 169).

RANGE India east to S China and Taiwan, south through the Philippines to Sulawesi, and south through the mainland to Malay Peninsula, Singapore, Sumatra, Java, Borneo, and east through the Sunda Islands to N Australia.

Kokol River Valley (QP)

Black Veined Tiger ■ *Danaus melanippus* (Cramer, 1777)
(Borneo race – *thoe*) [White Tiger]

HABITAT Lowland to hills, open spaces.   **ABUNDANCE** Moderately common.

DESCRIPTION Sexes similar. Forewing predominantly black with three broad white streaks, like the strokes of a painter's brush, radiating outwards. Two rows of angular white patches outer to that. Hindwing has more extensive white with blackened veins and double row of small white spots along margin. Underside similar. Male has pouch of scent scales on hindwing visible as a dark smudge. Note that the Borneo race differs significantly from most others across the region by entirely lacking any orange colour.

SIMILAR SPECIES One of eight species of tiger butterfly, all of which have black stripes on a pale ground colour. However, the pale areas of the wing surfaces are bright white, whereas most others have a grey or bluish tint. In male the all-black forewing-tip containing only a single white spot is distinctive.

HABITAT AND HABITS Found in open spaces, including around villages, farms and orchards; also in grassy areas or along sunlit margins of forests. Visits flowers for nectar. Flight slow and leisurely. In India recorded as migratory.

LARVAL FOOD PLANT Apocynaceae (oleander and milkweed family). On *Gymnema* and *Tylophora* spp. in Java. Also on Moraceae, *Ficus*, in Malay Peninsula.

RANGE India to S China, and south to Malay Peninsula, Sumatra, Java, Borneo, Palawan, the Philippines and Sulawesi.

Kokol River (CP)

Yellow Glassy Tiger ■ *Parantica aspasia* (Fabricius, 1787)

(Borneo race – *aspasia*)

HABITAT Lowland to hills, edge of forest.   **ABUNDANCE** Moderately common.

WINGSPAN /2–80mm

Poring (HP)

DESCRIPTION Sexes similar. Exhibits the typical warning colours of a bold black pattern on a pale background. Conspicuous flush of yellow extending from base of hindwing to black outer margin is distinctive. Ground colour pale bluish-grey. Hindwing well rounded, forewing more slender and elongated in male than in female.

SIMILAR SPECIES One of eight similar looking tiger butterflies, but distinguished from all others by the extensive flush of yellow. Also mimicked by female of the pierid Wanderer (p. 62), which resembles it closely in both appearance and flight.

HABITAT AND HABITs Flies in the open under the full sun at the edge of the forest or along forest trails. Also found in open grassland. Slow, unhurried flight. Visits wayside flowers such as Snakeweed *Stachytarpheta indica* (p. 170), pictured above, for nectar. Feeds with wings folded back. Male comes to wet ground for water. Kazuhisa Otsuka recorded that it 'sometimes appears in swarms'.

LARVAL FOOD PLANT Apocynaceae (oleander and milkweed family), and recorded on *Gymnema* spp. in Malay Peninsula and *Tylophora* spp. in the Philippines.

RANGE S Myanmar, Thailand, to Vietnam and south to Malay Peninsula, Singapore (very rare), Sumatra, Java, Bali, Borneo and Palawan.

Kinabalu Tiger ■ *Parantica crowleyi* (Jenner-Weir, 1894)

HABITAT Mountains, along ridges.   **ABUNDANCE** Local, not uncommon.

Mount Alab (CP)

DESCRIPTION Sexes similar. Bold pattern of broad pale streaks on a black background and submarginal double row of small white spots typical of the Danainae. Underside similar.

SIMILAR SPECIES One of eight species of tiger, but can be distinguished by two physical features and the habitat. Firstly, it is considerably larger than all other similar-looking species. Secondly, the two long, narrow square-ended longitudinal pale streaks towards the forewing apex are distinctive. Thirdly, it is predominantly montane.

HABITAT AND HABITS Found along mountain ridges. Although generally flies in tree canopy, also sometimes comes down to trails. Energetic with a powerful flight. Enjoys sunshine. Photographed taking mineral-rich moisture from a rocky cliff face. So far recorded on Mt Kinabalu and Mt Alab in Sabah, and Mt Mulu and Mt Murud in Sarawak, where it is the most common butterfly found at around 2,000m. Major C. M. Enriquez (1925) wrote: 'on the windswept ridge of Kamburonga [Mt Kinabalu, 2,000m] … Whitehead spent six weeks in 1887 and it is here he caught his highest altitude butterfly and that I also caught mine 38 years later – *Danaida crowleyi*'.

LARVAL FOOD PLANT Not recorded. Most likely on Apocynaceae (oleander and milkweed family) or Moraceae (fig, mulberry and jackfruit family), as other danainid butterflies.

RANGE Endemic to Borneo.

WINGSPAN 100–127mm

Grey Glassy Tiger ■ *Ideopsis juventa* (Cramer, 1777)
(Borneo race – *kinitis*)

HABITAT Coastal areas, seashore and islands.

ABUNDANCE Locally common.

DESCRIPTION Sexes similar. Exhibits typical black and white warning colouration. Has very fine black markings along veins, particularly on hindwing. Broad black border to both forewing and hindwing, within which there is a double row of small white spots. The extensive white areas of the wings have a definite pale bluish tint.

SIMILAR SPECIES One of eight species of tiger, but has the most extensive pale areas on the wings and the narrowest darkening along the veins.

HABITAT AND HABITS Found at the edges of wooded areas close to the seashore and in similar habitat on islands. Flight slow. Tends to fly low down close to the

Karambunai (HP)

ground, sometimes settling on a low twig or on leaf litter. May be seen visiting flowering grasses and flowers for nectar.

LARVAL FOOD PLANT Apocynaceae (oleander and milkweed family). In Malay Peninsula on *Gymnema*, *Pergularia odoratissima* and *Telosma cordata*. Also recorded on Piperaceae (pepper family), *Piper longum*.

RANGE Malay Peninsula, Borneo, the Philippines, Sulawesi to New Guinea and Solomon Islands, Sumatra, Java, and islands east to Alor.

Karambunai (HP)

Blue Glassy Tiger ■ *Ideopsis vulgaris (Butler, 1874)*
(Borneo race – *interposita*)

HABITAT Lowland to hills, edge of forest.   **ABUNDANCE** Moderately common.

DESCRIPTION Sexes similar. Exhibits the typical bold patterning of the tiger butterflies, with well-defined, broad pale streaks and stripes on a dark background and a submarginal border of a double row of pale spots. Streaks and spots are white, faintly tinted grey-blue.
SIMILAR SPECIES One of eight tiger species. Almost identical to the Dark Glassy Tiger *Parantica agleoides* of the same habits and habitat, but distinguished by long white streak in forewing cell being bisected, leaving a 'U'-shaped white patch mid-forewing.
HABITAT AND HABITS Typically found at the forest margin flying in sunshine. Lively. Flight fast but intermittently stops to rest briefly. Feeds on nectar, with sometimes numerous individuals feeding together. Takes moisture from the surface of damp concrete or wooden boardwalk. Kazuhisa Otsuka recorded that it sometimes appears in swarms.
LARVAL FOOD PLANT Apocynaceae (oleander and milkweed family), particularly on *Gymnema* elsewhere.
RANGE S Myanmar, Thailand, east to Hainan Island, south to Malay Peninsula, Singapore, Borneo, Palawan, Sumatra, Java and Sunda Islands east to Alor.

Samboja, Kalimantan (HP)

Mangrove Tree Nymph ■ *Idea leuconoe* (Erichson, 1834)
(Borneo race – *nigriana*)

HABITAT Seashore, islands.   **ABUNDANCE** Generally rare, but locally common.

DESCRIPTION Sexes similar. Large butterfly heavily marked with intricate black pattern on a white ground colour, including dark-dusted veins. Broad, irregular black border to both wings – broadest at forewing apex – contains white spots. Black markings are mostly angular in shape, rather than the rounded spots of other similar species.

Maratua (HP)

SIMILAR SPECIES Least common of four similar-looking species that occur in Borneo. Distinguished by location. Also has the greatest area of black on the wings and the most angular black markings. See also the Tree Nymph (p. 76).

HABITAT AND HABITS Inhabits coastal areas of the mainland and islands. Found in mangroves and back-mangrove habitat. Generally, floats high among the trees but descends occasionally. Feeds on nectar. Sometimes seen resting with wings outspread on low vegetation in sun or sun-dappled shade in forest clearings or along wooded pathways.

Rare throughout its range, but even on small islands populations can be large.

LARVAL FOOD PLANT Not recorded in Borneo; elsewhere on Apocynaceae (milkweed family), *Parsonsia alboflavescens* and *P. spiralis*.

RANGE Malay Peninsula, Singapore (very rare), Sumatra, Java, Borneo, Palawan, the Philippines, Taiwan and Okinawa (Ryukyu Islands, Japan).

Maratua Island (HP)

Tree Nymph ■ *Idea stolli* (Moore, 1883)
(Borneo race – *virgo*) [Ashy-white Tree Nymph]

HABITAT Forest, lowland to hills.   **ABUNDANCE** Moderately common.

Sepilok (CP)

DESCRIPTION Sexes similar. Very large and conspicuous. Overall the palest ashy-grey, almost white, with wings marked with large black spots in a uniform pattern and veins dark dusted. Forewing elongated and narrow, and hindwing slightly diamond shaped rather than rounded – not easy to see when in flight. Female slightly darker than male, with dark brown spots on a buffy-white background.

SIMILAR SPECIES The most common of four very similar-looking species in Borneo. See also the more heavily marked Mangrove Tree Nymph (p. 75).

HABITAT AND HABITS Found in primary forest and occasionally at forest edge. Flies high in the forest canopy, sometimes descending to visit flowers for nectar. Flies in a leisurely fashion, with each powerful wingbeat followed by a floating phase. R. Morrell wrote in *Common Malayan Butterflies*, 1960: 'Their timeless and ghostly movement high up in the shade of the canopy is one of the memorable sights of the Malayan jungle ...' Courtship dynamic, and consists of male and female swirling together like leaves in an eddy of wind. The Malay name for *Idea* species is *surat*, meaning a letter.

LARVAL FOOD PLANT Apocynaceae (oleander and milkweed family), especially *Gymnema*, on *Aganosma cymosa* in Malay Peninsula.

RANGE Malay Peninsula, Singapore, Sumatra, Java, Borneo and Jolo (Sulu archipelago).

Spotted Big Crow ■ *Euploea camaralzeman* (Butler, 1866)
(Borneo race – *scudderii*) [Malayan Crow]

HABITAT Lowland to hills, forest, forest edge.   **ABUNDANCE** Not uncommon.

DESCRIPTION Sexes differ. Large. Male overall dark brown both above and below.
Underside has double row of uniformly sized, small white spots along margin of both wings,
with a few scattered spots inner to that. Similar above, with slightly less spotting. Female
paler brown and much more heavily spotted both above and below.

SIMILAR SPECIES One of 12 crow butterflies (*Euploea*) found in Borneo, distinguished
by its large size and numerous well-defined, equal-sized small white spots distributed across
outer part of both wings. The slightly larger and much rarer *E. phaenareta* (not illustrated)
has spots more diffuse and unequal in size.

HABITAT AND HABITS Can be seen at the edge of the forest flying under the full sun.
Settles frequently, usually on dark surfaces. The photo shows the butterfly taking moisture
from a painted surface, presumably attracted by some trace element in the paint. Visits
flowers for nectar. The larval food plant renders both the larva and the adult butterfly toxic
to predators. Flies slowly unless disturbed.

LARVAL FOOD PLANT Moraceae (fig and mulberry family); Apocynaceae (milkweed
and oleander family).

RANGE S Myanmar, Thailand east to Vietnam, south to Malay Peninsula, Singapore (very
rare), Sumatra, Java, Borneo, Palawan and N Philippines.

Tabin (HP)

Spotted Black Crow ■ *Euploea crameri* (Lucas, 1853)
(Borneo race – *crameri*)

HABITAT Lowlands, forest edge, secondary growth.   **ABUNDANCE** Not uncommon.

DESCRIPTION Sexes similar but female paler than male. Male has dark brown underside. Forewing has six prominent white spots of uneven size at apex with the mid spot oval and clearly the largest. Scattering of small white spots mid-wing. Hindwing has single row of small white spots along margin, with the fourth one down slightly indented. Also cluster of small white spots mid-wing. Darker brown above – almost black, minimally marked by spots only at forewing apex and hindwing margin.

SIMILAR SPECIES *E. modesta* (not illustrated) is smaller with forewing apical spots more uniform in size. *E. midamus* (not illustrated) has blue gloss to basal area of forewing and full series of small marginal spots on forewing.

HABITAT AND HABITS Found at the margins of lowland forest or in secondary growth, including mangrove, coastal areas and inland. Often seen at the forest edge in bright sunshine. Flies strongly and moderately fast. Attracted to damp concrete and human sweat on clothing for mineral-rich moisture.

LARVAL FOOD PLANT Apocynaceae (milkweed and oleander family); recorded on *Parsonsia alboflavescens* and *P. helicaudra* in Malay Peninsula.

RANGE N. India, Bangladesh and Myanmar, to Malay Peninsula, Singapore, Sumatra, Java, Bali, Borneo and Palawan. Recorded as more common in Singapore than in Malay Peninsula.

Sungai Wain, Balikpapan (HP)

Striped Blue Crow ■ *Euploea mulciber* (Cramer, 1777)
(Borneo race – *portia*)

HABITAT Forest edge, lowlands to highlands.   **ABUNDANCE** Moderately common.

♀ *Tabin* (CP)

DESCRIPTION Sexes dissimilar. Male striking, with upperside of forewing a startling shade of bright iridescent blue that glints as he flies. Otherwise overall dark brown with a scattering of diffuse bluish-white spots across forewing. Female overall brown. Forewing has scattered white spots and subtle blue gloss on upperside. Hindwing brown streaked with white, most heavily on underside.

SIMILAR SPECIES One of 12 crow species in Borneo, but male has stronger blue on forewing than any other. Also mimicked by the day-flying moth *Cyclosia midamia* (see Mimicry, p. 22). Female similar to tigers, especially the Blue Glassy Tiger (p. 74), but distinguished by having spots not stripes on forewing.

HABITAT AND HABITS Found along forest margins and in open spaces, including roads, within the forest. Robust. Flies under the full sun with a swift and strong flight. Takes moisture from the ground and from concrete surfaces. Visits flowers. Migratory. Females less often seen than males.

LARVAL FOOD PLANT Moraceae (fig and mulberry family). Elsewhere also recorded on Apocynaceae (oleander and milkweed family), Aristolochiaceae (birthwort family) and Convolvulaceae (bindweed family).

RANGE SE India, Nepal, Bhutan, Myanmar, S China to Taiwan, south to Thailand, Malay Peninsula, Singapore, Sumatra, Java, Borneo, the Philippines and Sunda islands to Alor.

♂ *Temburong* (HP)

Magpie Crow ■ *Euploea radamanthus* (syn. *E. diocletianus*) (Fabricius, 1793)
(Borneo race – *lowii*)

HABITAT All elevations, forest edge, rocky streams.   **ABUNDANCE** Not uncommon.

Maliau (HP)

DESCRIPTION Sexes broadly similar. Male below dark brown with large white patch mid-forewing and a few prominent white streaks in basal area of hindwing. Also double row of bluish-white submarginal spots, largest at the apex. Above velvety bluish-black with similar pattern. Female similar but dark brown, with more white streaking on hindwing, especially underneath, and submarginal spots pure white.

SIMILAR SPECIES One of 12 species of crow (*Euploea*) in Borneo, but the large white patch mid-forewing is distinctive. Toxic to predators and mimicked by one female form of the non-toxic Indented Nymph (p. 125), which, however, has fewer white streaks and a wavy edge to the hindwing (see also Mimicry, p, 22).

HABITAT AND HABITS Found at all elevations, at the forest edge, along forest roads and river valleys, and in open grassland, although female keeps within the forest and is more rarely seen than male. Visits flowers for nectar. Also attracted to human sweat, animal waste and carcasses for minerals. Males come to damp ground for moisture. Can be attracted by dried plants of *Heliotropium indicum*.

LARVAL FOOD PLANT Moraceae (fig and mulberry family).

RANGE N India, Nepal, Myanmar, through continental Southeast Asia south to Langkawi, Malay Peninsula, Singapore, Natuna islands, Sumatra, Java, Bali, Borneo and Palawan.

Small Crow ■ *Euploea tulliolus* (Fabricius, 1793)
(Borneo race – *aristotelis*) [Dwarf Crow]

HABITAT Forest edge, coastal to hills, islands.   **ABUNDANCE** Not uncommon.

DESCRIPTION Sexes similar. Ground colour dark brown, with female slightly paler than male. Underside has a double row of small white spots along margin of both wings, with inner row extended round to follow inward curve of wing edge. Single white spot mid-forewing. Spots on under forewing more prominent and extensive in female than in male. Forewing above has submarginal row of bluish-white spots, increasing in size towards apex. Hindwing unmarked except for one or two small, faint white spots.

SIMILAR SPECIES One of 12 species of toxic crow (*Euploea*) in Borneo. Of these, the Small Crow is the smallest and has the least white spotting.

HABITAT AND HABITS Found in sunny areas at the edge of the forest, where it flies about actively, but also in open, grassy terrain and on larger islands. Typically perches for a while in a prominent position, such as on a bare twig or large, flat leaf, with the wings held back. Feeds on nectar. Males sometimes come to damp ground for moisture.

LARVAL FOOD PLANT Moraceae (fig and mulberry family). Also recorded on Apocynaceae (oleander and milkweed family) in China.

RANGE SE China, Taiwan, south to Malay Peninsula, Singapore, Sumatra, Java, Bali, Borneo, Palawan, the Philippines, east to New Guinea and Pacific islands, south to NE Australia.

Karambunai (CP)

Common Palmfly ■ *Elymnias hypermnestra* (Linnaeus, 1763)
(Borneo race – *nigrescens*)

HABITAT Gardens, plantations, forest edge.   **ABUNDANCE** Common.

DESCRIPTION Sexes similar, with female paler than male. Male underside rusty-brown with faint greyish striations, small white spot at upper margin of hindwing (absent in some individuals), and mottled white semi-circular 'thumbprint' at forewing apex. Wings have scalloped outer margin. Male blackish-brown above with row of diffuse light blue spots in a band across forewing apex. Female has paler bluish forewing spots above and a few whitish submarginal spots on hindwing. Very variable.

SIMILAR SPECIES At rest underwing virtually indistinguishable from that of the Multi Palmfly (p. 84), which, however, is rarer and inhabits primary forest or occasionally forest edge.

HABITAT AND HABITS Throughout the lowlands wherever palms occur, from edge of forest, to secondary growth, parks, gardens and oil-palm plantations. Settles with wings closed. Male holds a territory and perches on a large, prominent leaf, often in full sunshine, a metre or two high and may be seen at the same location on successive days. Visits rotting fruits and tree sap to feed.

LARVAL FOOD PLANT Recorded on Arecaceae (palms) across its entire range, including on *Cocos nucifera* (Coconut), *Elaeis guineensis* (Oil Palm) and *Areca catechu* (Betel Nut).

RANGE India, Sri Lanka, east through SE China to Taiwan, south to Malay Peninsula, Singapore, Sumatra, Java, Borneo and the Lesser Sunda Islands.

Mulu (HP)

Blue Lined Palmfly ■ *Elymnias nesaea* (Linnaeus, 1764)
(Borneo race – *hypereides*) [Tiger Palmfly]

HABITAT Forest edge, lowlands to hills.   **ABUNDANCE** Uncommon.

DESCRIPTION Sexes similar, with female paler than male. Underside entirely mottled in black, grey and rust. Outer edges of both wings noticeably scalloped (not clearly visible in photo due to marginal wing damage). Above has veins heavily darkened with brown against a pale ground colour, giving an overall striped effect similar to that of the tigers of the Danainae (pp. 69–74), which it mimics, although the flight is very different. Towards the forewing-tip the pale areas between the dark stripes are flushed with blue in male and violet in female.

HABITAT AND HABITS Flies swiftly and high at the edge of the forest in the lowlands and hills, preferring shade to sunlight. Chooses dark surfaces to land

Kipandi Enclosure (HP)

on, settling with wings back, so the cryptically coloured underside enables it to remain undetected.

LARVAL FOOD PLANT Arecaceae (palms); records elsewhere include *Calamus* (rattan), *Cocos nucifera* (Coconut) and *Areca catechu* (Betel Palm).

RANGE Thailand, Malay Peninsula, Sumatra, Java, Borneo, the Philippines (Sulu archipelago).

The *Elymnias* are interesting because of the high incidence of mimicry. Of the nine species found in Borneo, five have brown wings, many with blue gloss, like the crows (*Euploea*), one female has dark spots on a white background like the *Ideopsis*, and another is red and yellow, mimicking a jezebel (*Delias*, Pieridae).

Multi Palmfly ■ *Elymnias penanga* (Westwood, 1851)

(Borneo race – *konga*) [Pointed Palmfly]

HABITAT Forest, forest edge, lowland to hills.   **ABUNDANCE** Uncommon.

Poring (HP)

DESCRIPTION Sexes differ. Female is polymorphic, occurring in two forms in Borneo. Photo shows both male (right) and female. Male underwing rusty-brown with greyish striations, small, squarish white spot on upper edge of hindwing, and indistinct white triangular smudge at apex of forewing. Male above has deep violet-blue forewing streaked with pale blue. Female pale form (shown here) has mostly mottled underwing with silver-white on a dark background; dark brown above with large white panel on forewing and larger white area on hindwing. The other female form is like the male but paler.

SIMILAR SPECIES Closely resembles the Common Palmfly (p. 82) but less abundant. Distinguished by having less wavy outer wing-margin and entirely blue forewing above, and otherwise by preference for dark jungle-edge habitat.

HABITAT AND HABITS Found at the edges of primary forest where there is thick foliage and little light, staying in the shade or semi-shade. Male holds a territory and may be seen perched on a prominent leaf at about 2m height. Easily disturbed and swiftly retreats to the deeper shadows.

LARVAL FOOD PLANT Arecaceae (palms).

RANGE Thailand, Malay Peninsula, Singapore (Pulau Ubin, rare), Sumatra and Borneo.

Malayan Owl ■ *Neorina lowii* (Doubleday, 1849)
(Borneo race – *lowii*)

HABITAT Lowland to hill forest.   **ABUNDANCE** Local, not uncommon.

Poring (CP)

DESCRIPTION Sexes similar, with female slightly paler than male. One of the largest of the Satyrinae. Easily recognizable, with distinctive pattern. Black-brown above with large, irregularly shaped, creamy-white patch running from forewing to hindwing on outer edge. Row of four small white spots running up outer forewing to tip clearly visible when at rest. Short, blunt tails to hindwing and excavated forewing. Two large eyespots very faint in Borneo race. Underside same but paler.

HABITAT AND HABITS Found in lowlands to hills. Generally, occurs deep in the forest and prefers shade or partial shade, but sometimes seen at the edge of forest clearings or

along forest paths. Strong, swift flight usually about a metre above ground level. Typically settles with wings open on a low, prominent perch. Male will chase off other butterflies. Becomes more active towards evening. Feeds on rotten fruits.

LARVAL FOOD PLANT Poaceae (grass family), particularly *Dendrocalamus giganteus*, Giant Bamboo, and probably also other bamboos.

RANGE Malay Peninsula, Sumatra, Borneo and Palawan (but absent from Java).

Temburong (QP)

SIR HUGH LOW
The Malayan Owl is named after Sir Hugh Low (1824–1905), a British colonial administrator in Borneo and a naturalist. He made the first documented ascent of Mt Kinabalu in 1851 and the mountain's highest peak is named after him. He also collected specimens of plants and butterflies, including *Rhododendron lowii*.

Common Bush Orange ■ *Mycalesis anapita* (Moore, 1858)
(Borneo race – *fucentia*) [Tawny Bush Brown]

HABITAT Lowland forest, forest edge.   **ABUNDANCE** Common.

Overwing: note large eyespot is well clear of the dark border

DESCRIPTION Sexes similar with female paler than male. Underside pale orange traversed by two thin, dark orange lines. Three, sometimes four, submarginal eyespots on forewing and seven on hindwing. Upperside orange with broad black margin to forewing widest at tip and partial narrow black margin to hindwing. Single larger white-pupiled eyespot just inner to black border mid-forewing, and row of four small submarginal eyespots on hindwing. Female lacks thin black border to hindwing.

SIMILAR SPECIES The most common of four species. Most like *M. patiana*, but this has eyespot on forewing above partially obscured by dark border, and underneath is darker orange, whereas the Common Bush Orange has a diffuse pale halo around each marginal eyespot. The Kinabalu Bush Orange (p. 88) is essentially montane with a wider dark border to both wings above. *M. fusca* is all brown above with a well-defined pale ring around each eyespot below.

HABITAT AND HABITS Found in lowland forest up into the foothills. Flies low in partly shaded areas of the forest. Often settles on low undergrowth, usually with wings closed, or occasionally fully open basking in the sunshine. Feeds on overripe fruits.

LARVAL FOOD PLANT Poaceae (grass family).

RANGE S Thailand, Malay Peninsula, Sumatra and Borneo.

Mulu (HP)

Banded Bush Brown ■ *Mycalesis horsfieldi* (Moore, 1892)
(Borneo race – *hermana*)

HABITAT Forest edge, open country.   **ABUNDANCE** Not uncommon.

Sungai Wain (HP)

DESCRIPTION Sexes similar with female paler than male. Evenly rounded wings. On the underside a distinct thin, outwardly diffuse white band traverses both forewing and hindwing. Complete row of small to medium submarginal eyespots, with five on forewing and seven on hindwing. Ground colour mid-brown although slightly paler around eyespots. Dark brown above with single large, semi-obscured eyespot mid-forewing, the female usually having one or two eyespots apparent on the hindwing as well.

SIMILAR SPECIES One of six very similar bush browns (*Mycalesis*) that all have a thin, pale line across both wings and a row of submarginal eyespots. Distinguished by having five eyespots on forewing beneath, with fourth slightly larger.

HABITAT AND HABITS Found from the lowlands to the hills. Flutters close to the ground at the forest edge, along forest trails or on the edges of fields. Settles on low vegetation in the sunshine, most often with wings closed. Feeds on rotting fruits.

LARVAL FOOD PLANT Poaceae (grass family), including *Imperata cylindrica*, *Oryza sativa* (rice) *Saccharum officinarum* (sugar cane), grasses, padi and bamboo.

RANGE Malay Peninsula (very rare outside of Johore and the Tioman islands), Sumatra, Java, Bali, Borneo, Palawan, Sulawesi and the Philippines (very rare).

Kinabalu Bush Orange ■ *Mycalesis marginata* (Moore, 1881)
(Borneo race – *pitan*)

HABITAT High mountains, forest.

ABUNDANCE Locally common.

Kinablau Park HQ (CP)

DESCRIPTION Sexes similar, with female larger than male. Upperside predominantly orange with broad black border to both wings only slightly wider at forewing apex. Darkened wing-bases. On hindwing a row of submarginal eyespots is mostly obscured by the dark border with some eyespots just visible. Underside pale orange traversed by two thin, reddish-orange lines. Row of small submarginal eyespots, five on forewing and seven on hindwing.

SIMILAR SPECIES The Common Bush Orange (p. 86) and M. *patiana*, but both are lowland species, whereas the Kinabalu Bush Orange occurs only at high altitudes.

HABITAT AND HABITS Occurs in montane forest. Often seen at the forest edge. Habitually settles but usually only briefly in a sunny spot along a path, basking with wings spread flat. Easily disturbed and flies off quickly in a zigzag flight, moving up into the treetops or disappearing off into the forest. Evidently adapted to tolerate montane weather and flies in varying conditions, from sunny to cloudy, windy and even light rain. Relatively common at Mount Kinabalu Park HQ along the ring road.

LARVAL FOOD PLANT Poaceae (grass family).

RANGE Borneo and Sumatra.

Dark Brand Bush Brown ■ *Mycalesis mineus* (Linnaeus, 1758)
(Borneo race – *macromalayana*)

HABITAT Forest edge, grassy places.   **ABUNDANCE** Common.

DESCRIPTION Sexes similar, with female paler and larger than male. Underwing mostly uniform mid-grey-brown with a distinct narrow, outwardly diffuse white band traversing both wings. Submarginal series of eyespots of varied size. Entirely darker grey-brown above with a single large, white-pupiled eyespot mid-forewing.

SIMILAR SPECIES The most common of several species. Distinguished by more unequal-sized eyespots on underside, particularly on forewing. Most like M. *perseus*, which, however, is darker and has roughly equal-sized submarginal eyespots on the underside, and above has more or less obscure forewing eyespot. White band slightly more prominent in the Dark Brand Bush Brown.

HABITAT AND HABITS Found throughout the lowlands wherever grasses grow, from forest clearings and forest edge to cultivated land and gardens. Flies low with a slow, jerky flight, preferring areas of shady undergrowth. Feeds at rotting fruits and tree sap. Males frequent damp patches. Active throughout the day.

LARVAL FOOD PLANT Poaceae (grass family); elsewhere (Malay Peninsula, China, India) noted on *Oryza sativa* (rice) and *Saccharum officinarum* (sugar cane), among others.

RANGE India, Sri Lanka to S China, south to Malay Peninsula, Singapore, Sumatra, Java, Bali, Borneo, the Philippines and east to New Guinea.

Tabin (CP)

Lilac-banded Bush Brown ■ *Mycalesis oroatis* (Hewitson, 1864)

HABITAT Lowland to hill forest.   **ABUNDANCE** Not common.

DESCRIPTION Sexes similar, with female slightly paler and larger than male. Underwing has a narrow, pale, luminescent outwardly diffuse lilac band crossing both wings and a submarginal row of eyespots, two on the forewing widely separated, and seven on the hindwing of more or less equal size except for the fifth down being larger. Ground colour soft mid-brown – the colour of fallen leaves on the forest floor. Dark reddish-brown above with a diffuse darker border and a single eyespot on forewing. Female orange-brown above with more prominent forewing eyespots.

SIMILAR SPECIES Of the few similar banded bush browns, recognized by the narrow, faintly lilac-purple band on the underwing and eyespot pattern.

HABITAT AND HABITS Found in undisturbed areas of lowland forests. Tends to stay low in the dimly lit undergrowth, settling on leaf litter, stones or fallen logs. Comes to overripe fruits.

LARVAL FOOD PLANT Not recorded. Note, however, that the overwhelming majority (28/29) of *Mycalesis* species in the Oriental region have been recorded on Poaceae (grass family) including grasses, bamboos and padi (rice), with one species on Zingiberaceae (ginger family), so grasses are the most likely food plants.

RANGE Malay Peninsula, Sumatra, Java and Borneo.

Poring (CP)

Purple Bush Brown ■ *Mycalesis orseis* (Hewitson, 1864)
(Borneo race – *borneensis*)

HABITAT Forest, forest edge, lowland to hills. · · · **ABUNDANCE** Moderately common.

Poring (HP)

DESCRIPTION Sexes similar. Male underwing has broad, outwardly diffuse, lilac-tinged band and submarginal eyespots, five on forewing and seven on hindwing. Male has dark purple sheen above, to otherwise dark brown wings. Large black patch of androconia (pheromone-dispersing scales) mid-hindwing is hard to discern. Female below similar to male. Female above paler mid-pinkish-brown, with no purple gloss and with band and eyespots of underside pattern showing faintly. Note that in Borneo race, eyespots are more uneven in size than in Malay Peninsula race, and underside forewing is lilac washed.
SIMILAR SPECIES One of several similar-looking bush browns distinguished by band on underside being broad, outwardly diffuse and distinctly lilac tinted, and having five eyespots on forewing beneath, with fifth distinctly largest.
HABITAT AND HABITS Found in the lowlands to the hills either within the darker reaches of the forest or at the forest edge. Prefers shady locations near areas of grass. Tends to fly low, often close to the forest floor, and typically rests on low vegetation with wings closed, revealing underwing.
LARVAL FOOD PLANT Poaceae (grass family), including grasses, padi and bamboo.
RANGE Thailand, Malay Peninsula, Singapore, Sumatra, Borneo and Palawan (absent from Java).

Utang Resident ■ *Coelites euptychioides* (C. & R. Felder, 1867)
(Borneo race – *euptychioides*) [Purple-streaked Catseye]

HABITAT Undisturbed lowland forest.　　　**ABUNDANCE** Not uncommon.

Sungai Wain (HP)

DESCRIPTION Sexes similar, with female slightly larger and paler than male. Underneath striking, with conspicuous large eyespot towards tip of hindwing and luminescent pale lilac-blue band traversing both wings. Row of smaller submarginal black, cream-ringed eyespots set in a pale lilac-blue border. The number of eyespots varies between individuals, although the largest is always present. Ground colour pinkish-brown. Dull brown above with a bluish-violet glossed area at the hindwing tip.

HABITAT AND HABITS Inhabits undisturbed lowland forest, and found in the undergrowth in the darkest recesses of the forest. Perches with wings closed on a prominent leaf, typically at about a metre height, but if approached flies off deeper into the forest. Described as rare with regard to the Malay Peninsula, but not uncommon in Borneo in suitable habitat. The word Utang is an alternative for the Malay *utan*, meaning forest.

LARVAL FOOD PLANT Not recorded in Borneo. Recorded on Arecaceae (palm family), *Calamus* (rattan palms) in Malay Peninsula.

RANGE Malay Peninsula, Sumatra and Borneo.

Striped Ringlet ■ *Ragadia makuta* (Horsfield, 1829)
(Borneo race – *umbrata*) [Brown-banded Ringlet]

HABITAT Lowland to hill forest.   **ABUNDANCE** Moderately common.

DESCRIPTION Sexes similar, except female slightly larger than male, with more rounded wings. Unmistakable. Underside has series of broad, chocolate-brown bands on a cream background, creating a bold, striped pattern. Entire row of silver-centred eyespots along wing margin – eight on forewing and seven on hindwing. Entirely pale greyish-brown above, with underside pattern showing through faintly. Antennal club orange tipped with black.

HABITAT AND HABITS Inhabits lowland and hill forest, where it can be seen in the shade or semi-shade along forest paths and streams, often

Mulu (HP)

flitting between sunlit patches on the forest floor. Tends to stay low and not travel far. Settles with wings closed. Sips water from damp ground such as sandy or gravelly surfaces. Habitually perches on a prominent leaf at about 1–2m height, where its bold stripes make it highly visible. Conversely, in dappled sunlight on a pebbly surface, the same pattern may be disruptive and act as camouflage (p. 20).

LARVAL FOOD PLANT Peacock Fern, Selaginellaceae.

RANGE Malay Peninsula, Sumatra, Java and Borneo (but absent from Palawan).

PEACOCK FERN Malay: Paku Merak
Selaginella willdenowii Selaginellaceae
A larval food plant of the Striped Ringlet. A relative of the ferns, this is a low, rather straggling plant to about 1m in height. Each stem has a row of larger, more obvious leaves on either side, but also a row of much smaller leaves along the stem – allowing the maximum capture of

light. The leaves appear bluish, however, the blue colour is not due to pigment, but to the structure of the cell surface, which selectively absorbs the red light rays needed for photosynthesis. The convex cell surface also acts as a lens to concentrate light on the chlorophyll. This plant is thus well adapted to life on the dimly lit forest floor.

Small Ring ■ *Ypthima fasciata* (Hewitson, 1865)
(Borneo race – *fasciata*) [Malayan Six Ring]

HABITAT Lowland to hills, forest edge.   **ABUNDANCE** Moderately common.

DESCRIPTION Sexes similar, with female slightly larger than male, paler and with more rounded wings. Underside has three indistinct, dark brown bands on a white-streaked buff background. On hindwing outer band contains an orderly row of seven small eyespots more or less equally sized and uniformly spaced. Forewing has one large, double-pupiled eyespot at apex. Overwing mirrors underside, but is so obscured that it gives an overall brown impression.

(Note that common names refer *only* to the number of eyespots on *underside* of *hindwing*, and conjoined or double eyespots are counted as one eyespot.)

SIMILAR SPECIES One of three similar *Ypthimas* (ring butterflies). Overwing is the most dingy, with eyespots barely discernible. Underwing pattern similar to that of the Five Ring *Y. baldus*. However, the latter has less defined dark bands and submarginal eyespots are arranged in pairs that are non-aligned.

HABITAT AND HABITS Found along sunlit margins of lowland forest. Flies at bush height and often settles on a prominent perch, such as a broad leaf in sun or partial shade, with wings folded back. Comes to flowers for nectar.

LARVAL FOOD PLANT Poaceae (grass family).

RANGE Malay Peninsula, Singapore, Sumatra and Borneo.

Sungai Wain (HP)

Common Three Ring ■ *Ypthima pandocus* (Moore, 1858)
(Borneo race – *sertorius*)

HABITAT Wayside, grassland, forest edge.   **ABUNDANCE** Common.

DESCRIPTION Sexes similar, with female paler than male and slightly larger. Mid-grey-brown above, with one large, yellow-ringed, double-pupiled eyespot towards forewing apex. Hindwing has one medium and one small eyespot towards tip. Underneath mid-brown lightly streaked with white, especially on hindwing. Pale underside to hindwing noticeable both at rest and in flight. Forewing has one large eyespot as above.

Kokol River Valley (CP)

Hindwing has three bold, medium-sized eyespots, giving rise to the common name.

SIMILAR SPECIES Three similar species of ring butterflies (*Ypthima*) occur in Borneo, which are all distinguished by the number of eyespots on the *underside* of the *hindwing*.

HABITAT AND HABITS Common and widespread. Found at all altitudes, from the coast to the mountains, including at Kinabalu Park HQ. Occurs in a variety of habitats, from grassy verges to forest tracks. Flies low among tall grass or low bushes. Rests with wings open or closed. Generally, sun loving but adaptable, and on mountains flies in grey windy weather and even during light rain. Visits flowers for nectar.

LARVAL FOOD PLANT Poaceae (grass family), including *Imperata cylindrica* (Lallang Grass) and *Paspalum conjugatum* (Carabao Grass).

RANGE Malay Peninsula, Singapore, Sumatra, Java, Borneo, Palawan, the Philippines (in the latter it is treated by some authors as a distinct species, *Y. sempera*).

Karambunai (HP)

Yellow Band ■ *Xanthotaenia busiris* (Westwood, 1858)
(Borneo race – *burra*) [Yellow-barred Pan]

HABITAT Lowland to hill forest.   **ABUNDANCE** Moderately Common.

Sungai Wain (HP)

DESCRIPTION Sexes similar, with female larger than male. Readily identified. On underside prominent broad, pale yellow band traversing forewing is distinctive. Otherwise yellow-brown shading to dark rust-brown at forewing-tip and traversed by thin, wavy rust-brown lines. Three large, pale silvery-grey eyespots on hindwing look more like fungus than false eyes. Rufous-brown above with darker forewing-tip traversed by yellow band and single white spot. Long antennae, about 70 per cent of the length of the forewing.
HABITAT AND HABITS Typically found in undisturbed lowland primary forest, preferring open forest with low-growing gingers, such as along riverbanks. Flies low within shady undergrowth. Settles among the leaf litter of forest floor with wings folded back, revealing underwing. Well camouflaged by muted colouring and mottled markings resembling fungi on leaves. Active early and late (crepuscular). Feeds on fallen forest fruits.
LARVAL FOOD PLANT Zingiberaceae (ginger family), particularly *Zingiber*.
RANGE NE India, S Myanmar, S Thailand, Malay Peninsula, Sumatra and Borneo.

Graceful Faun ■ *Faunis gracilis* (Butler, 1867)
(No races described)

HABITAT Forest, lowland to hills.   **ABUNDANCE** Locally common.

DESCRIPTION Sexes similar. Medium sized with rounded wings. Underwing tawny orange-brown with two thin, dark irregular lines like watermarks that extend across forewing to hindwing in two widely separated arcs. Forewing has submarginal row of small white dots, one of which is developed into a white-pupiled black eyespot with an outer tawny-orange ring. Hindwing has five white submarginal spots, the first and last of which are fully formed eyespots. Above entirely unmarked tawny orange-brown, with slightly darker dusty-brown along margins.

SIMILAR SPECIES One of four species of faun butterflies in Borneo. Distinguished from the most similar Banded Faun (p. 98) by the richer orange-brown colouring and presence of an eyespot on the forewing underside.

HABITAT AND HABITS Occurs in lowland forest. Tends to stay low, settling with wings closed on the forest floor, where it is well camouflaged, or on low vegetation, where it is more conspicuous. Feeds on fallen forest fruits. Takes moisture from damp surfaces. In the dimly lit forest the two hindwing eyespots are conspicuous, but the subdued colour of the rest of the butterfly, and the real eye, make its form and size obscure.

LARVAL FOOD PLANT Arecaceae (palm family).

RANGE Malay Peninsula, Sumatra and Borneo

Mulu (HP)

Banded Faun ■ *Faunis stomphax* (Westwood, 1858)
(Borneo race – *stomphax*)

HABITAT Lowland to hill forest.   **ABUNDANCE** Moderately common.

DESCRIPTION Sexes similar but variations occur in both sexes. Medium sized with rounded wings. Underside generally charcoal, sometimes paler dusky brown. Hindwing traversed by two widely separated, thin, dark wavy lines like watermarks, and has a submarginal row of five white dots, the first and last of which are full white-centred black eyespots. Forewing has a transverse thin, dark line and a submarginal row of three small white dots towards the apex. However, some individuals have a row of six white spots, the third and last being full eyespots. Some females have a very distinct, medium-width white band partially or fully across the forewing – hence the common name. Overwing entirely dark reddish-brown.

SIMILAR SPECIES One of four faun butterfly species in Borneo. Distinguished by thin dark line across forewing, which is always present – otherwise by eyespot pattern. Larger and darker than the otherwise similar Graceful Faun (p. 97).

HABITAT AND HABITS Found in lowland forests. Flies close to the ground among the sparse undergrowth of the shady forest. Frequently settles on leaf litter or on low vegetation with wings closed before taking flight again. Feeds on overripe fallen fruits on the forest floor. Active throughout the day.

LARVAL FOOD PLANT Arecaceae (palm family), in Palawan on Pandanaceae (pandan and screwpine family).

RANGE Borneo, Sumatra and Palawan.

Mulu (HP)

Big-eyed Jungle Lady ■ *Taenaris horsfieldii* (Swainson, 1820)
(Borneo race – *occulta*)

HABITAT Forest, lowland to hills.   **ABUNDANCE** Uncommon, local.

DESCRIPTION Sexes similar, with female larger and paler than male. Unmistakable. Hindwing underneath charcoal-grey at base; outer half white with two very large, conspicuous eyespots, each with a black centre and orange-yellow outer ring. Forewing entirely grey-buff. Pale grey-buff above with a smaller area of white on outer half of hindwing and only one large eyespot apparent. Forewing elongated and hindwing heavily rounded.

HABITAT AND HABITS Occurs in lowland to hill forest. Prefers damp, shady but open forest. Tends to settle with wings closed or half open. Quite sedentary and perches for

Poring (CP)

some time on low to medium-height vegetation in the half-light among the forest trees.

LARVAL FOOD PLANT Not recorded in Borneo. On *Smilax*, Smilacaceae (sarsaparilla family) in Malay Peninsula and the Philippines.

RANGE Malay Peninsula, Sumatra, Java, Borneo and Palawan (no longer in Singapore). This is a rare example of a Papuan genus spreading from east to west across Wallace's Line.

Palm King ■ *Amathusia phidippus* (Linnaeus, 1763)
(Borneo race – *phidippus*)

HABITAT Gardens, plantations and forest.   **ABUNDANCE** Moderately common.

Kota Kinabalu (CP)

DESCRIPTION Sexes similar. Large. Variable. Underside has transverse bands of soft brown, pearly-grey and pinkish-buff of varying widths, with a prominent central band. Hindwing has two large, widely separated eyespots. Lobed tip with two small dark spots often missing, presumably due to predator attack (see p.21). Overall dark brown above with female tawny-yellow at margins. Pale form (*A. gunneryi*) also occurs.
SIMILAR SPECIES The most common of five species. Distinguished by underwing having less contrasting stripes than those of the other species. They are also forest dwellers and all have a more pronounced dark central band with white or cream edging.
HABITAT AND HABITS Found in the lowlands in proximity to coconut or other palms. Occurs in village gardens, along the seashore, in plantations and forested areas. By day rests with wings closed on the underside of foliage. Feeds on overripe fruits. Active early morning and evening (crepuscular). Attracted to lights at night much like a moth.
LARVAL FOOD PLANT Arecaceae (palms). On Coconut, Oil and Nipah palms in Malay Peninsula; on Sago, Sealing Wax, Sugar Palm and Musaceae in the Philippines.
RANGE India, Myanmar, east to Vietnam and south to Malay Peninsula, Singapore, Sumatra, Java, Borneo, Palawan, the Philippines and Sulawesi.

Dark Blue Jungle Glory ■ *Thaumantis klugius* (Zinken, 1831)
(Borneo race – *lucipor*) [Blue Palm King]

HABITAT Undisturbed forest, lowland to hills.   **ABUNDANCE** Uncommon.

DESCRIPTION Sexes dissimilar. Large with rounded wings. Male underside, visible at rest, is chocolate-brown with a scattering of subtle silver-grey smudges, looking like mould on a leaf, two small eyespots that appear as pale crescents, a narrow diffuse pale band across the forewing, and an indistinct lilac-brown marginal border. Upperside, glimpsed only in flight, is a brilliant dark iridescent blue against a dark brown background. Female larger than male. Similar to male underneath, but more differentiated with larger, well-defined eyespots, paler forewing-band and paler border. Mid-brown above with iridescent dark blue at wing-bases and pale zigzag submarginal border.

SIMILAR SPECIES Female underside very like that of the Blue-banded Jungle Glory (p. 103) but pattern not so well defined.

HABITAT AND HABITS Occurs in lowland to hill forest. Usually near streams. Stays low, settling on leaf litter on the forest floor, where it is well camouflaged. Generally sedentary but if disturbed 'will spring to life beneath our feet' (Morell, 1988) and flies off, revealing the startling blue overwing that 'flashes darkly and mysteriously', before settling again.

LARVAL FOOD PLANT Arecaceae (palm family).

RANGE S Thailand, Malay Peninsula, Singapore, Sumatra, Java and Borneo.

Sungai Wain (HP)

Dark Jungle Glory ■ *Thaumantis noureddin*
(Westwood, 1851) (Borneo race – *chatra*) [Pointed Orange Spotted Forester]

HABITAT Forest, lowland to hills.   **ABUNDANCE** Not uncommon.

DESCRIPTION Sexes differ. Male has dark reddish-brown underside with some scattered white flecking. Two large hindwing eyespots appear only as faint crescents. Thin, dark submarginal line outwardly dusted with lilac frosting. Forewing slightly angled just below apex. Hindwing has bluntly pointed tip. Male above black-brown with tawny-yellow along outer forewing and slight purple-blue gloss at wing-base. Female larger and paler, and has a golden-yellow band above, across forewing, and a significant purple-blue sheen to basal area of wings.

SIMILAR SPECIES Female similar to the female Dark Blue Jungle Glory (p. 101) above but has less blue sheen and hindwing pointed not rounded.

HABITAT AND HABITS Inhabits interior areas of lowland and hill forests. Most often found near streams. Tends to fly low, settling with wings closed on the forest floor among leaf litter or tangled undergrowth, where its sombre colouring and sedentary habit make it hard to spot. Visits damp patches and fallen fruits.

LARVAL FOOD PLANT Unrecorded.

RANGE Malay Peninsula, Sumatra and Borneo.

Danum (CP)

Blue-banded Jungle Glory ■ Thaumantis odana (Godart, 1824)
(Borneo race – panwila)

HABITAT Undisturbed forest, lowland to highlands.   **ABUNDANCE** Uncommon.

Sungai Wain (HP)

DESCRIPTION Sexes similar. Large, with female larger than male. Underside, visible at rest, cryptic in shades of brown from chocolate to buff, with wing-bases frosted with pearly-grey. Hindwing has two large, distinct eyespots, typical of the genus, one fully ringed and one appearing as a crescent. Forewing has a distinctive cream-coloured transverse band. Female (illustrated) slightly paler than male, with submarginal band on both wings lilac tinged rather than dull brown. Brown above with a diffuse, pale blue iridescent band across forewing. Single small white fleck at forewing apex is distinctive.

SIMILAR SPECIES Underside very like that of the female Dark Blue Jungle Glory (p. 101), which, however, is darker and has pale forewing band more sharply defined.

HABITAT AND HABITS Found in undisturbed forests, preferring dry, relatively open forest. Stays low, settling on the leaf litter of the forest floor, where its colouring in shades of grey and brown blends with the fallen leaves. Generally sedentary but if disturbed flies off, the brilliant blue on the forewing above flashing in the jungle dark. Does not fly far before resettling on the carpet of fallen leaves. Most active at dusk.

LARVAL FOOD PLANT Not recorded. On Arecaceae (palm family) in captivity.

RANGE S Thailand, Malay Peninsula, Sumatra, Java and Borneo.

Blue Duffer ■ *Discophora necho* (C. & R. Felder, 1867)
(Borneo race – *cheops*)

HABITAT Lowland forest.   **ABUNDANCE** Uncommon.

Mulu (HP)

DESCRIPTION Sexes differ. Large. Female (illustrated) has underwing in shades of pinkish-buff and soft brown. Two large, faint eyespots on hindwing and dark-edged, diffuse, broad pale band that traverses both wings. Forewing squared and hindwing rounded. Female dark brown above with broad orange band across forewing and a few orange spots along hindwing margin. Male has underside similar to female in shades of buff and brown with indistinct banding. Male greyish-blue above with blue-white marks in a broad band across forewing. Hindwing has pale-bordered, circular black patch of androconia (pheromone [scent] producing scales).

SIMILAR SPECIES In the not dissimilar Common Duffer *D. sondaica* (not illustrated), male has angled hindwing and female lacks orange band on over-wing.

HABITAT AND HABITS Inhabits lowland forest and sometimes seen at forest edge. Shy and secretive. Generally, settles with wings closed among foliage at a height of 3–4m. Swift and strong in flight. Comes to rotting fruits and feeds with wings closed, making it well camouflaged among fallen leaves on the forest floor.

LARVAL FOOD PLANT Poaceae (grass family), on *Bambusa* (bamboo) in Malay Peninsula.

RANGE Malay Peninsula, Sumatra, Java, Borneo, Palawan and the Philippines.

Common Nawab ■ *Polyura athamas* (Drury, 1773)
(Borneo race – *uraeus*)

HABITAT Hills, edge of forest.   **ABUNDANCE** Moderately common.

DESCRIPTION Sexes similar, with female larger than male. Settles with wings back and underwing showing. Above, a broad white panel runs across the central area from forewing to hindwing, surrounded by dark border. One large white spot towards forewing apex. Central panel appears greenish-white underneath and surrounding border is grey-brown with a few pale flecks and paler still in female. Hindwing scalloped, forewing indented. Two short but distinct tails to hindwing.

SIMILAR SPECIES Six species of the *Polyura* genus occur in Borneo, of which three – this one, *P. moori* and *P. hebe* – have a very similar underwing pattern and are hard to distinguish. In the Common Nawab, top of pale central panel is smoothly rounded, and submarginal row of well-defined white dashes on hindwing helps with identification.

HABITAT AND HABITS Male has a strong, very swift flight, seeming to swoop in suddenly out of nowhere. Perches high on foliage in full sun when resting. Frequents margins of forests and nearby dry river beds, gravel roads or other open spaces. Attracted to animal excrement and damp ground.

LARVAL FOOD PLANT Leguminosae, including *Acacia*, *Albizia* and *Caesalpinia* (peacock flower family) recorded in Malay Peninsula.

RANGE India, Nepal, Myanmar, Thailand, S China, to Malay Peninsula, Sumatra, Java, Borneo and the Philippines.

Samboja, Kalimantan (HP)

Malayan Lacewing ■ *Cethosia hypsea* (Doubleday, 1847)
(Borneo race – *hypsea*)

HABITAT Forest, edge of forest, lowlands to hills.   **ABUNDANCE** Moderately common.

Kipandi (HP)

DESCRIPTION Sexes similar but colours more subdued in female than in male. Forewings above black crossed by irregular broad white band. Hindwings predominantly a strong reddish-orange with a broad black border. Wings have serrated edges. Underwing has irregular pattern of red, orange, white, black and pale blue, with a black and white zigzag pattern along margin accentuating scalloped wing edge. Colours are a warning to predators that this species is unpalatable.

SIMILAR SPECIES Closely resembles *C. biblis* in the same genus but has larger white area on forewing above and only two pale bands on hindwing below.

HABITAT AND HABITS Flies at the edge of the forest open to sunshine at bush height. Generally active, fast flying and difficult to approach, but occasionally rests on foliage in exposed position with wings spread. Feeds on nectar with wings back, displaying dazzling underwing.

LARVAL FOOD PLANT Passifloraceae (passionflower), especially *Adenia* spp., feeding on the tendrils or young shoots. Has been recorded on *A. macrophylla* in Borneo.

RANGE S Myanmar, S Thailand, Malay Peninsula, Singapore, Borneo, Sumatra, Java and Palawan.

Kipandi (HP)

Cruiser ■ *Vindula dejone* (Erichson, 1834)
(Borneo race – *dejone*)

HABITAT Lowlands to hills, edge of forest.   **ABUNDANCE** Moderately common.

DESCRIPTION Sexes differ. Large, with female larger than male. Male tawny-orange, with mid-wing golden, but darker at wing-base and wing margin. Two distinct submarginal eyespots on hindwing. Wings bordered by double narrow, dark scalloped line. Pinkish-beige beneath. Short tails. Female has broad white band running down centre of both wings. Inner to this greenish-grey, and outer wing orange-brown. Two prominent eyespots on hindwing. Paler and more uniform beneath.

♂ *Mulu (CP)*

SIMILAR SPECIES V. *erota* is 'almost indistinguishable' (Morrell) and for more than 100 years the two *Vindula* species were regarded as a single species. V. *erota* flies in the highlands and is slightly larger than this species, with shorter tails.

HABITAT AND HABITS Forest, forest edge and nearby habitation. Male bold and swift in flight, sometimes flying low down. Comes to puddles, damp ground by streams and drainage ditches, settling with wings spread flat. Also attracted to sweat on clothing, rucksacks and exposed skin. Female seen at flowers or flying high up at the forest edge, investigating potential egg-laying sites.

♀ *Karambunai (HP)*

LARVAL FOOD PLANT Passifloraceae (passion flower and granadillo family), *Passiflora quadrangularis*. Larvae feeding on the leaves of this genus are resistant to the many toxins the plants produce, but become toxic to predators.

RANGE Malay Peninsula, Singapore, Borneo, Palawan, the Philippines, Sulawesi, Moluccas, Sumatra, Java, Bali and islands to Timor.

Island Rustic ■ *Cupha arias* (C. & R. Felder, 1867)
(Borneo race – *arias*)

HABITAT Islands, seashore.   **ABUNDANCE** Locally common.

Maratua, Kalimantan (HP)

DESCRIPTION Sexes similar. Medium sized with rounded wings. Orange above, with a broad, irregular transverse cream to pale yellow band to forewing and broad black apex. Hindwing has triple border of thin, wavy black lines and inner to that a prominent row of dark spots. Underneath patterned as above but duller and paler. Butterflies of this species found on Maratua (shown here) have indistinct forewing band and are significantly paler than those featured by K. Otsuka (1988)) – and may be a different race.

SIMILAR SPECIES Hard to tell apart from the Rustic (opposite). Distinguished primarily by location – the Island Rustic is an island specialist, whereas the Rustic is found throughout the lowlands on the mainland. Furthermore, in the Island Rustic the inner margin of the broad pale forewing band is more or less smooth except for a single small projection, whereas in the Rustic the edges of the pale band are noticeably irregular, including a double peaked projection.

HABITAT AND HABITS Confined to seashore and island habitats. Enjoys sun or partial shade. On Maratua Island, Kalimantan, is common and abundant, occurring in large colonies and rarely seen singly.

LARVAL FOOD PLANT Flacourtiaceae (Rukam family).

RANGE Borneo, the Philippines and Sulawesi.

Rustic ■ *Cupha erymanthis* (Drury, 1773)
(Borneo race – *erymanthis*)

HABITAT Lowland to hills, forest edge.   **ABUNDANCE** Moderately common.

DESCRIPTION Sexes similar. Medium sized with rounded wings. Tawny orange-brown above, appearing as dull brown to strongly orange depending on the light. Forewing has a wide, irregular cream transverse band and broad black apex. Hindwing has triple border of thin, wavy black lines. Underneath patterned as above but much paler.

SIMILAR SPECIES Almost identical to the Island Rustic (opposite), which, however, is much rarer and occurs only on islands and along the seashore.

HABITAT AND HABITS Found at the forest edge or in forest clearings from the lowlands to the hills. Often seen flitting about bushes in sun or shade at about 1–3m height. Very restless, constantly twisting and turning and opening and closing its wings, while moving around on foliage or on the ground. Flight typically in short bursts. Occasionally stops to bask. Males are territorial. Attracted to flowers and damp concrete. S. Igarashi & H. Fukuda (1997) report that: 'Interestingly, when a spider's silken cobweb is available spun between the leaf edges, very often the ovum is laid onto it. ... There have been 1–3 ova found on one filament.'

LARVAL FOOD PLANT Flacourtiaceae (Rukam family).

RANGE India, Sri Lanka to S China, Hong Kong, Taiwan, south to Malay Peninsula, Singapore, Borneo, Palawan, Sumatra, Java, east through Lesser Sunda Isles to Alor.

Samboja, Kalimantan (HP)

Banded Yeoman ■ *Paduca fasciata* (C. & R. Felder, 1860)
(Borneo race – *fasciata*)

HABITAT Forest, edge of forest.   **ABUNDANCE** Uncommon, local.

DESCRIPTION Sexes similar. Strong pattern that is distinctive. Ground colour mid-brown but darker towards wing margins. Well-defined, broad cream band starting at mid-forewing runs across centre of both wings. Outer to this brown ground colour alternates with two more bands of cream markings in a scalloped pattern, finishing with a dark brown border at the wing margin.

HABITAT AND HABITS Found in primary forest from the lowlands to the hills. Prefers shade or semi-shade and damp, and may be found at the margins of forests, on secluded forest paths or near rivers or streams. Has a feeble flight and tends to stay low. Settles with wings open flat. Visits flowers for nectar and has also been recorded feeding on animal excrement and carcasses. Details of life history and breeding habits unknown. Also recorded as 'very local' in Malaya and the Philippines.

LARVAL FOOD PLANT Flacourtiaceae, *Hydnocarpus*, Myrtaceae (myrtle, eucalyptus, clove and guava family), *Eugenia*.

RANGE Malay Peninsula, Sumatra, Java, Borneo, Palawan and the Philippines.

Poring (CP)

Clipper ■ *Parthenos sylvia* (Cramer, 1775)
(Borneo race: *borneensis*)

HABITAT Lowland to hills, edge of forest.   **ABUNDANCE** Moderately common.

DESCRIPTION Sexes similar. Large. A handsome butterfly with a striking pattern in iridescent colours. Central area of forewing has bold lateral stripes of green on black, replaced by lilac on black on hindwing. On forewing an irregular row of large white patches form a band. Hindwing has a strong submarginal zigzag pattern in bronze. Underside pattern

Sepilok (QP)

more subdued and paler. Distinctive and unmistakable.

HABITAT AND HABITS Found at forest edges. Often seen taking nectar from flowers and is especially attracted to *Lantana*. It may, for instance, be found on the plants outside the Information Centre at Sepilok Forest Reserve. Also feeds on ripe fruits both on the tree and fallen to the ground. Enjoys sunshine and is often sighted basking on a prominent leaf in the sun with outspread wings. Has a powerful gliding flight. Flies at all levels, from shrubs to canopy.

Danum (HP)

LARVAL FOOD PLANT Passifloraceae (passionflower and granadillo family). Elsewhere also recorded on Menispermaceae (curare family).
RANGE India, Sri Lanka, Myanmar, east to the Philippines, south to Malay Peninsula, Sumatra, Java, Borneo, Sulawesi, New Guinea east to the Solomon Islands. Recorded as rare throughout most of its range, including Malay Peninsula, but moderately common in Borneo and occurs at Danum, Sepilok, Tabin and Poring.

Commander ■ *Moduza procris* (Cramer, 1777)
(Borneo race – *agnata*)

HABITAT Hill forest.   **ABUNDANCE** Not uncommon.

DESCRIPTION
Sexes similar, with female larger and paler than male. Upperside dark reddish-brown with a broad, irregular white band running down centre of both forewing and hindwing. In strong sunlight wings may appear almost black. In contrast, underside is much lighter, with pale greenish-grey on basal half of wings, and intricately

Poring (CP)

patterned in black, grey and rust on outer part. The broad white band is still apparent.
HABITAT AND HABITS Inhabits forested areas in the hills. Found at the forest margin, in clearings and along forest paths and roads, especially near streams and rivers. Flies swiftly with a strong, gliding flight, frequenting sunlit areas at the edge of the forest. Basks with wings spread flat. Feeds on rotten fruits and tree sap. Also attracted to animal excrement and damp patches.
LARVAL FOOD PLANT Rubiaceae (coffee, *Ixora* and gardenia family); additionally Salicaceae (willow family) and Myrtaceae (myrtle, clove and guava family) in Borneo.
RANGE India, Sri Lanka, Myanmar, S China, to Hainan, south to Thailand, Malay Peninsula, Singapore, Sumatra, Java and islands east to Flores, Borneo, Palawan and Sulu islands (the Philippines).

Poring (CP)

Orange Staff Sergeant ■ *Athyma cama* (Moore, 1858)
(Borneo race – *ambra*)

HABITAT Highland to montane, forested areas.   **ABUNDANCE** Uncommon.

DESCRIPTION Sexes very different. Male above has broad, white horizontal stripes on a black background. Only one white band on forewing. Hindwing has two white bands, one thick and a second very thin. Small, obscure reddish-orange dot at apex of forewing is distinctive. Underneath has the same pattern, but white on brown and with a second forewing stripe. Female has broad orange bands on a dark brown background and a transverse orange band across forewing apex.

SIMILAR SPECIES One of 11 species. Male distinguished by lack of second white stripe on forewing. Female similar to female of *A. nefte*, form *neftina* (not illustrated), but larger and darker with reduced orange on wings above.

HABITAT AND HABITS Montane species found in forested areas, but often seen in the open in full sun such as along forest tracks. Prefers rocky sites. Flight strong and low. Comes to damp ground. Can be found around Kinabalu Park HQ.

LARVAL FOOD PLANT Not recorded in Borneo. On species of *Glochidion* (Euphorbiaceae) (spurge family) in India and China.

RANGE NE India, Myanmar, east to S China and Taiwan, south through mainland to Malay Peninsula, Sumatra and N Borneo.

Kinabalu Park HQ (CP)

Greater Lascar ■ *Pantoporia dindinga* (Butler, 1879)
(No races described)

HABITAT Forest edge, all elevations.   **ABUNDANCE** Uncommon.

DESCRIPTION Sexes similar, although female is more subdued in colouring than male. Broad orange horizontal stripes on black-brown background. Underside has corresponding pattern of buff-coloured bands alternating with grey edged with black. Orange-tipped antennae and orange legs.

SIMILAR SPECIES There are five *Pantoporia* and four *Lasippa* species in Borneo that all closely resemble each other. *P. dindinga*, the Greater Lascar, male, is distinguished by double row of two fine submarginal lines on the forewing that are grey – not orange – and the inner one being inwardly indented mid-wing, a rounded orange patch on the outer forewing that is separated from the main orange band, and the forewing orange streak being deeply notched. Note that for many years butterflies of the *Pantoporia* and very similar *Lasippa* group were included within the larger *Neptis* genus but are now classed as separate genera.

HABITAT AND HABITS Found at all elevations but particularly in the hills at the forest edge and along wide forest tracks. Habitually suns itself on low vegetation in the open.

LARVAL FOOD PLANT Not recorded (but note the majority of other *Pantoporia* species in the region are all recorded on Leguminosae (pea and mimosa family).

RANGE Myanmar, Thailand, Malay Peninsula, Sumatra and Borneo.

Kokol Ridge (CP)

Southern Sullied Sailor ■ *Neptis clinia* (Moore, 1872)

(Borneo race – *ila*) [Clear Sailor]

HABITAT Open areas at forest edge.   **ABUNDANCE** Not uncommon.

Poring (CP)

DESCRIPTION Sexes similar, with female larger than male. Broad white horizontal stripes on a black background above. Underside has same pattern but ground colour mid-brown. Orange-tipped antennae. The bold black and white stripes warn off predators.

SIMILAR SPECIES One of many similar species, of which four are especially hard to distinguish. The Southern Sullied Sailor has the narrowest gap in the long white forewing streak, and the triangle tip tapers to the narrowest point. *N. duryodana* has only four large, squarish submarginal white spots on the forewing and two much smaller ones. *N. magadha* has only three large, rectangular submarginal white spots on the forewing. See also the Common Sailor (p. 117), probably the most common *Neptis* and easy to distinguish by the orange-brown colour of the underwing.

HABITAT AND HABITS Found at low to moderate elevations in sunny locations at the edge of the forest. Has a slow, gliding flight and tends to stay low. Good views when at rest as habitually settles with wings open on a prominent leaf or rock, or other perch in full sunshine.

LARVAL FOOD PLANT Not recorded in Borneo. Elsewhere (Vietnam and Hong Kong) recorded on Leguminosae (peas, beans and mimosa family), particularly *Dalbergia* species.

RANGE India, Myanmar, Thailand to S China, south through Southeast Asian mainland, to Malay Peninsula, Sumatra, Java, Bali, Borneo and Palawan.

Chocolate Sailor ■ *Neptis harita* (Moore, 1875)
(Borneo race – *mingia*) [Brown Sailor, Dingiest Sailor]

HABITAT Forest, forest edge.   **ABUNDANCE** Uncommon.

Mulu (HP)

DESCRIPTION Sexes similar. Dark brown above with paler horizontal bands of pinkish-buff. The pale bands are more slender, obscure and diffuse than the white bands on the black sailors. Pattern replicated underneath but is paler, so that broad band on hindwing appears almost white.

SIMILAR SPECIES Probably the most common of three closely related brown sailor species, the others being *N. omeroda* and *N. ilira*. Described as a confusing and difficult group of species by Corbet & Pendlebury (1992) with apparently three strains '… descended from a recent common ancestor which … have been unable to interbreed on coming together again …' The only distinguishing feature is a crescent-shaped as opposed to squarish spot on the outer forewing above, which in practice is often not clear and in any event is barely discernible in the field.

HABITAT AND HABITS Found from the lowlands to the hills. Frequents open spaces near the forest edge. Habitually rests on low-growing vegetation such as bushes or tall grasses or on the ground. Basks in full sun with wings spread flat. Low, gliding flight.

LARVAL FOOD PLANT Moraceae (mulberry and fig family). Elsewhere on Urticaceae.

RANGE NE India, Myanmar, Thailand, east to Vietnam and south to Malay Peninsula, Singapore, Sumatra and Borneo.

Common Sailor ■ *Neptis hylas* (Linnaeus, 1758)
(Borneo race – *sopatra*)

HABITAT Farmland, roadside verges, forest edge.   **ABUNDANCE** Common.

Tabin (CP)

DESCRIPTION Sexes similar, with female larger than male. Broad white horizontal stripes on a black background above. Underneath has the same pattern as above, but ground colour is orange-brown and white markings are edged in black. White-tipped antennae. Thorax has blue-green sheen. Male has speculum (glossy sexual patch) on upper hindwing.

SIMILAR SPECIES The most common of several species. Distinguished by the large gap in the white forewing streak and by the orange-brown ground colour underneath.

HABITAT AND HABITS Most abundant in the lowlands. Found in open, sunlit habitats including farms, villages, roadside verges and wide forest tracks. Habitually basks on low vegetation in full sun with wings spread flat. Often slowly opens and closes its wings while perched. If disturbed usually settles again on a similar perch nearby. Slow, low gliding flight. Active throughout the day.

LARVAL FOOD PLANT Fabaceae (pea and mimosa family), Malvaceae (mallow family). Across the Oriental region recorded on more than 20 species of Fabaceae, as well as plants from several other families.

RANGE India east to S China, Hong Kong, Taiwan, Ryukyu Islands (Japan), south to Malay Peninsula, Singapore, Sumatra, Java, Borneo and Sunda islands east to Tanimbar,

Samboja, Kalimantan (HP)

Red Spotted Duke ▪ *Dophla evelina* (Stoll, 1790)
(Borneo race – *magama*) [Redspot Duke]

HABITAT Forest, lowland to hills.

ABUNDANCE Not uncommon.

Tabin (HP)

DESCRIPTION Sexes similar, with female larger and paler than male. Large. Upperside dusty mid-brown – the colour of fallen leaves. Bright red spot midway on leading edge of each forewing. In the dim light of the forest floor, only the two red spots are visible, appearing like the eyes of a mammal. Predominantly mid-grey-blue underneath with a few small red spots. Forewing noticeably outcurved towards tip.

SIMILAR SPECIES The Pearl Necklace (opposite) is smaller, with a prominent chain of white spots above and overall paler beneath.

HABITAT AND HABITS A butterfly of the forest, staying in the shadows, but may be seen at the forest edge or in clearings as it feeds on rotting fruits such as the Elephant Apple *Dillenia indica* pictured. In flight glides low, 1–3m above the ground, among the trees, habitually settling with wings open on leaf litter, fallen tree trunks or fallen fruits. Males territorial. It has been reported to travel more than 2km, and also to live for up to three months (P. Houlihan, 2012).

LARVAL FOOD PLANT Ebenaceae (ebony and persimmon family), Euphorbiaceae (tapioca and rubber family), Anacardiaceae (mango family) and Fagaceae (oak family).

RANGE India, Sri Lanka, Myanmar, Thailand to Vietnam, south to Malay Peninsula, Sumatra, Java, Borneo, Palawan, the Philippines and Sulawesi.

Tabin (HP)

Pearl Necklace ■ *Bassarona dunya* (Doubleday, 1848)
(Borneo race – *monara*) [Great Marquis]

HABITAT Lowland to hill forest.   **ABUNDANCE** Not uncommon.

DESCRIPTION Sexes similar, although female is larger than male. The colour of milky coffee above. Distinctive wing pattern with string of 16 conspicuous, creamy-white, dark-edged spots running across both wings in a long loop – perfectly described by the common name. Also has a narrow, glossy purple-blue border along leading edge of forewing that shows more in certain lights.

Mulu (HP)

Pale greenish-blue underneath, with faint spots mirroring overwing pattern.
SIMILAR SPECIES B. *teuta* is darker brown with larger white spots forming a continuous band. The Red Spotted Duke (opposite) is larger, without any white spots, and has a strongly outwards curved forewing-tip.

Mulu (HP)

HABITAT AND HABITS Occurs primarily in lowland forest. Flies in the semi-gloom of the understorey with a strong flight, tending to stay low. Habitually settles on the ground with wings spread, where it is well camouflaged among fallen forest leaves. Feeds on rotting fruits on the forest floor and may be seen feeding at the forest edge or in forest clearings. If disturbed rapidly retreats to the cover of the undergrowth.
LARVAL FOOD PLANT Not recorded.
RANGE S Myanmar, Thailand, Malay Peninsula, Sumatra, Java, Borneo and Palawan.

Streaked Baron ■ *Euthalia alpheda* (Godart, 1824)
(Borneo race – *parta*)

HABITAT Lowland to hill forest.   **ABUNDANCE** Uncommon.

DESCRIPTION Sexes dissimilar. Male above dark brown traversed by obscure broad bands of darker brown. Wings angular. Underneath tawny-brown with white marks on forewing at apex and mid-wing, and some darker brown striations. Female (shown) pinkish-buff above with five angular, pearly-white patches forming broad band mid-forewing and diffuse lilac-white patch at apex. The remainder has diffuse bands of alternating pale and dark buff. Underneath very pale bluish-white; more honey coloured towards wing-bases. Green proboscis.

SIMILAR SPECIES One of the least common of a large group of similar species.

HABITAT AND HABITS Frequents undisturbed lowland forest. Active in sunlit forest clearings, where it flies around settling on a variety of perches, from leaf litter, where it is well camouflaged, to green foliage, to fallen tree trunks. Rests with wings open in the sunshine. Strong flyer. Attracted to overripe fruits, and to damp wood for moisture.

LARVAL FOOD PLANT Not recorded in Borneo, but elsewhere recorded on Anacardiaceae (mango family), including *Mangifera indica* (Mango).

RANGE India, Myanmar, Thailand, Malay Peninsula, Sumatra, Java, Borneo and the Philippines.

♀ *Sungai Wain (HP)*

Horsfield's Baron ■ *Tanaecia iapis* (Godart, 1824)
(Borneo race – *ambalika*)

HABITAT Forest edge, lowlands to lower montane.   **ABUNDANCE** Moderately common.

DESCRIPTION Sexes differ substantially. Male above velvety blue-black with broad luminescent blue border to hindwing extending to forewing, then tapering to apex. Buff to brown underneath with a few dark brown striations. Female above pinkish-buff with pattern of white streaks radiating outwards. Female very variable, with some individuals having a diffuse lilac to blue band on the hindwing.

Sepilok (CP)

SIMILAR SPECIES The most common of several species. Male can be distinguished from all others with a blue hindwing border by the purity of the blue border, and from the most similar Malayan Count *T. godarti* by the narrow white edging outer to the blue.

HABITAT AND HABITS Occurs in forested areas at all elevations, from the lowlands to lower montane. Flies swiftly and low at the forest edge or in the understorey of open forest in areas of patchy sunlight. Settles on low foliage in the sun with wings open. Males defend a territory. Females more seldom seen. Comes to rotting fruits and also attracted to tree sap.

LARVAL FOOD PLANT Melastomataceae (medinilla family), including the Straits Rhododendron *Melastoma malabathricum* and Euphorbiaceae (spurge family) (see also p.167).

RANGE S Thailand, Malay Peninsula, Singapore, Sumatra, Java, Borneo and Palawan.

♀ *Poring (CP)*

Whitehead's Baron ■ *Euthalia whiteheadi* (Grose Smith, 1889)
(Borneo race – *whiteheadi*)

HABITAT Montane and submontane forest.　　　**ABUNDANCE** Uncommon, local.

♀, *Kinabalu Park HQ (CP)*

DESCRIPTION Sexes differ. Male has angular wings. Black-brown above. Forewing has seven small white dots towards apex. Hindwing has a partial green iridescent border, a single red dot at the tip, and a cluster of six red spots usually hidden by forewing. Female larger and more colourful than male. Ground colour dark coffee. Three large white patches form an irregular band across mid-forewing. Six large white spots at forewing apex. Broad, iridescent blue-green border on hindwing. Red dot at hindwing tip and a further six along margin. These may draw the attention of a predator away from the head and are sometimes missing as a result of predator attack.

SIMILAR SPECIES One of four similar-looking species, but the only montane one.

HABITAT AND HABITS Found in forested areas on mountains and surrounding hills such as Mt Kinabalu and the Crocker Range in Sabah, north Borneo. Tolerates cool temperatures and overcast conditions. Prefers habitat near streams. Male comes to damp ground. Rests with wings open on foliage or on the ground in open spaces. Both sexes are strong flyers.

LARVAL FOOD PLANT Loranthaceae (mistletoe family).

RANGE Thailand, Malay Peninsula, Sumatra, Java and Borneo.

JOHN WHITEHEAD

Whitehead's Baron is named after John Whitehead (1860–1899). Born in London and educated at the Edinburgh Institute, he developed an intense interest in natural history and became an intrepid pioneer and tireless collector of zoological specimens, exploring northern Borneo in the years 1884–1888, about 20 years after Wallace. Whereas Wallace had travelled eastwards down the archipelago visiting many remote islands, Whitehead focused on the interior mountains.

His foremost interest was in birds, and he collected in the region of 45 new species from Mt Kinabalu, three of which – known as 'Whitehead's trio' – are illustrated below. But he was also interested in and collected mammals, butterflies, beetles and reptiles, and he collected 16 new butterfly species from Mt Kinabalu.

After two previous unsuccessful attempts he finally reached the rocky summit of Mt Kinabalu on 11 February 1888, and returned to England a few months later. *The Exploration of Mount Kina-Balu* (1893), illustrated with his own colour plates, was his only major publication.

Whitehead travelled and collected in the Philippines in 1893–1896, and in 1899 in the mountainous interior of Hainan Island. He and his entire party were overcome with fever and he died on 2 June 1899 aged only 38. His dedication was formidable and he describes his motivation in the introduction to *Kina-Balu*: 'I did not visit these lands for the purpose of collecting hides and horns for my trophies, but rather the more lasting beauties of the East, and especially, if possible, to add some little everlasting stone to that ever increasing cairn of human knowledge …'

Whitehead's Trogon, male

Whitehead's Broadbill, male

Whitehead's Spiderhunter, male

Village Archduke ■ *Lexias pardalis* (Moore, 1878)
(Borneo race – *dirteana*) [Archduke]

HABITAT Lowland forest.   **ABUNDANCE** Moderately common.

Poring (CP)

DESCRIPTION Sexes differ greatly. Male above velvet-black with a sprinkling of golden-orange dots towards leading edge of forewing. Broad blue border to hindwing contains row of large black dots. Forewing has a subdued greenish-grey border tapering to apex. Underneath rusty-brown with light spotting. Female above entirely dark brown with rows of golden-yellow spots in a strong, regular overall pattern. Paler below with under-hindwing pale greenish-bluish-grey.

SIMILAR SPECIES The most common of several species. Distinguished from the most similar Black-tip Archduke *L. dirtea* by *orange* tip to black antennae. (Note that in *Lexias* species the hindwing blue border does not extend up to the wing edge.)

HABITAT AND HABITS A butterfly of lowland forests, preferring open forest and areas near villages. Has a swift gliding flight, tending to stay low. Settles with wings spread on the leaf litter of the forest floor, where the female is well camouflaged but the male is conspicuous. Feeds on decaying matter, including rotting fruits, animal droppings and carcasses.

LARVAL FOOD PLANT Clusiaceae (mangosteen family); widely reported on *Garcinia* species in India, Vietnam and Java).

RANGE NE India, Myanmar, Thailand, S China, to Hainan, south to Malay Peninsula, Singapore, Sumatra, Java, Borneo, Palawan and the Philippines.

♀ *Mulu (CP)*

Indented Nymph ■ *Euripus nyctelius* (Doubleday, 1845)
(Borneo race – *borneensis*) [Courtesan]

HABITAT Lowland to hills, forest edge.   **ABUNDANCE** Uncommon.

Lok Kawi, Kota Kinabalu (QP)

DESCRIPTION Sexes differ greatly. Male iridescent blue-black above, streaked and
spotted with white in a bold, orderly pattern. Hindwing has a squarish protrusion. Dark
brown underneath marked in white as above. Female considerably larger and occurs in
several different forms, all of which mimic the unpalatable crows (*Euploea*). Form *isina*
deep bluish-black above with a white patch mid-forewing, mimicking male of the Magpie
Crow (p. 80). Form *euploeoides* mimics the female of the Magpie Crow. A further form
mimics the Striped Blue Crow (p. 79).

SIMILAR SPECIES The 'models' from the crows (*Euploea*) described above.

HABITAT AND HABITS Occurs from the lowlands to the hills. Found at the margins
of the forest. Male can be seen in the open and although usually flies swiftly and high,
descends to wet ground for water and also attracted to sweat on clothing. Females flutter
slowly around low-growing vegetation, mimicking the behaviour of the crows, which they
resemble, and are less often seen than the males.

LARVAL FOOD PLANT Ulmaceae (elm family), *Trema orientalis*, Urticaceae (nettle and
Ramie Fibre family).

RANGE N India to S China and south to Malay Peninsula, Singapore, Sumatra, Java,
Borneo, Palawan and the Philippines.

Orange Mapwing ■ *Chersonesia rahria* (Moore, 1858)
(Borneo race – *rahria*) [Wavy Maplet]

HABITAT Lowland to hills, forest edge.   **ABUNDANCE** Moderately common.

Poring (CP)

DESCRIPTION Sexes similar, with female larger and paler than male. Small. Tawny-orange with four bands of medium width in a darker shade of orange-brown running across forewing to hindwing. First two bands edged in dark brown, while the third is a diffuse dark line and the fourth contains a row of dark dashes. The lines are similar to contour lines on a map – hence the common name. Forewing-tip has a dark indistinct smudge mottled with orange. Very small but distinct tail midway along hindwing margin.

SIMILAR SPECIES The most common of six similar species and has the least contrasting bands. On the forewing the third band curves inwards and the fourth band curves outwards at the same point to create a broad, rounded, paler patch

HABITAT AND HABITS Occurs in lowland to hills. Forest butterfly most usually seen at the forest edge or along wide-open forest tracks. Flight feeble. Can be seen in full sun settled with outspread wings. Also frequently settles on undersides of leaves with its wings open.

LARVAL FOOD PLANT Moraceae (fig and mulberry family); recorded on *Ficus racemosa* in Malay Peninsula.

RANGE N India to Malay Peninsula, Sumatra, Java, Borneo, Palawan, the southern Philippines and Sulawesi.

Blue Admiral ■ *Kaniska canace* (Linnaeus, 1763)

(Borneo race – *maniliana*)

HABITAT Highland to montane.   **ABUNDANCE** Uncommon.

DESCRIPTION Sexes similar. Distinctive. Upperside inky bluish-black with a contrasting broad mid-blue band running down centre of both wings. This is broader in female than in male. Wings ragged looking with an irregular wavy edge. Underside cryptically patterned in mottled browns and black, resembling a dead leaf.

HABITAT AND HABITS Occurs at higher altitudes, often along mountain ridges. Frequents open spaces surrounded by forest. Often settles on paths or on rocks in full sunshine with wings open. Flies off at great speed if disturbed. Habitually remains active throughout the afternoon even on cooler days. Male is territorial. Feeds on overripe fruits and tree sap.

LARVAL FOOD PLANT Liliaceae (lily family); elsewhere recorded on Smilacaceae (sarsaparilla family) in Malay Peninsula, and on Dioscorea (yam family) in India.

RANGE India, Sri Lanka east to China, Hong Kong and Japan, south through mainland to Malay Peninsula, Sumatra, Java, Borneo and the Philippines.

Mt Alab (HP)

With its ragged edged wings and mottled, camouflaged underside, the Blue Admiral is noticeably similar to the comma (*Polygonia*) butterflies of Europe and North America, which are generally orange-brown in colour. Previously considered to belong to the same genus, this species is now classed in a genus of its own (*Kaniska*).

Malayan Eggfly ■ *Hypolimnas anomala* (Wallace, 1869)
(Borneo race – *anomala*)

HABITAT Lowlands, forest edge.

ABUNDANCE Moderately common.

Maratua Island, Kalimantan (HP)

DESCRIPTION Sexes similar. Entirely dark purplish-brown with double row of small white spots along margins of both wings, less distinct in female than male. In some lights there appears a slight blue gloss on the upper surface of the female forewing. Variable.

SIMILAR SPECIES Mimics butterflies of the *Euploea* genus, known as the crows, which are distasteful to predators (p. 77). In Australia known as the Crow Eggfly (for mimicry, see also p. 22).

HABITAT AND HABITS Butterfly of bushy forest edge at low altitudes, from islands to seashore and inland. Often settles on a prominent leaf of low vegetation in the semi-shade, or on a path. Male displays territorial behaviour and if disturbed will settle again at the same spot or nearby. Breeds throughout the year. Larvae gregarious.

LARVAL FOOD PLANT Urticaceae (nettle family); *Pipturus* genus – recorded on *P. argenteus* in Borneo, Singapore, Thailand, elsewhere on *P. arborescens*.

RANGE The Philippines, Sulawesi, Palawan, southern Thailand, Malay Peninsula, Borneo, Sumatra, Java, and islands east to Timor (rare records from Hong Kong, Taiwan and northern Australia).

In 1979, while travelling in the Philippines, Gweneth Johnston was the first person to record the unique protective behaviour of the Malayan Eggfly butterfly. Gweneth Johnston had an interest in natural history from an early age. Born in South Africa she has lived and travelled throughout Southeast Asia, including Indonesia, Malaysia and Singapore. After moving to Hong Kong in 1972 she co-authored two significant reference books on the butterflies of Hong Kong, in 1980 and 1999 (see bibliography).

PROTECTIVE PARENTING – GUARDING HER EGGS

The unique behaviour of the Malayan Eggfly
Eggs are laid in a single cluster of 400–600 on the underside of a leaf. 'The female remains standing over the eggs for about seven days, without nourishment, until the eggs have hatched and the larvae dispersed to other leaves, and apparently may die in this position.' (Bascombe et al., *The*

Malayan Eggfly, H. Anomala, ♀ standing over her eggs (HP)

Butterflies of Hong Kong, 1999). The female drives off small ants that would otherwise devour her eggs by beating her wings. Guarding the eggs and young larvae has been found to increase the survival rate by up to 50 per cent but is ineffective against larger ants and parasitic wasps.

Our photos were taken on Maratua Island, East Kalimantan, Indonesia, along the side of a track where the favourite food plant, *Pipturus argenteus*, predominated.

There was a Malayan Eggfly with eggs on nearly every bush. This female guarding newly hatched larvae did not fly off even when the leaf was carefully held up to enable a better photo.

This behaviour is recorded in no other butterfly except *Hypolimnas antilope*, a closely related species of the adjacent Moluccas and New Guinea.

Malayan Eggfly, H. Anomala, ♀ guarding newly hatched larvae (HP)

Great Eggfly ■ *Hypolimnas bolina* (Linnaeus, 1758)
(Borneo race – *philippensis*)

HABITAT Lowland, open country.

ABUNDANCE Common.

♂ *Karambunai (HP)*

DESCRIPTION Sexes differ. Male deep blue-black above, with large, blue-tinged iridescent white egg-shaped spot in centre of each hindwing. Underside dark brown with broad transverse white band across both wings. Both sexes have a white patch at the forewing apex above. Female larger and more variable than male, occurring in several different forms (polymorphic) but all have a dark blue-black or brown background and a submarginal row of tiny white spots. One form has a large orange patch on the forewing.

SIMILAR SPECIES Some of the female forms mimic crows, *Euploea*.

HABITAT AND HABITS Found in sun or partial shade in a variety of open habitats, including gardens, villages, farms, roadside verges, secondary growth and forest edge. Visits flowers. Also feeds on rotten fruits. Male territorial, typically establishing a perch on low vegetation. Strong flyer and has been recorded taking part in migratory flights.

LARVAL FOOD PLANT Convolvulaceae (bindweed and morning glory family), including the Sweet Potato *Ipomoea batatas*, Acanthaceae (acanthus family) and Urticaceae (nettle and Ramie Fibre family), Amaranthaceae (amaranths family).

RANGE Madagascar, India, Sri Lanka, S China, Hong Kong, Taiwan, Japan (Ryukyu Islands), the Philippines, mainland to Malay Peninsula, Singapore, Borneo, Sulawesi, Sumatra, Java, New Guinea, Solomon Islands, Vanuatu to Easter Island, south to N and E Australia.

♀ *Tempasuk Plain (HP)*

Underwing, Karambunai (CP)

Grey Pansy ■ *Junonia atlites* (Linnaeus, 1763)
(Borneo race – *atlites*)

HABITAT Lowlands to hills, open grassy spaces.   **ABUNDANCE** Very common.

DESCRIPTION Sexes similar. Predominantly pale creamy-grey, although male upperside is tinged with lilac. More numerous eyespots than in the other pansies (*Junonia*), with a complete row of small but prominent eyespots of slightly unequal size along margins of both wings. The most developed of these are black crowned with orange. Underside paler.

HABITAT AND HABITS Found in lowlands, occasionally in the hills. Favours sunlit, open grassy spaces, including roadside verges, scrubland and equally around villages, cultivated land or at the forest edge. Typically seen perched on a prominent leaf at a low level in full sunlight with wings open flat. If disturbed flies off at speed but often returns to the same spot. Flight low and gliding. Visits flowers. Active throughout the day.

LARVAL FOOD PLANT Urticaceae (nettle family), Acanthaceae (acanthus family), particularly *Hygrophila*, Amaranthaceae (amaranth family), Scrophulariaceae (figwort and wightia family), Verbenaceae (lantana family). Note that females of *Junonia* species frequently lay their eggs in the vicinity of, rather than on, the larval food plants, and once hatched the larvae move to the actual food plant nearby. So eggs found on a plant may not signify that the larvae feed on that plant.

RANGE India, Sri Lanka, Myanmar, Thailand, S China, Hong Kong, the Philippines, south to Malay Peninsula, Singapore, Borneo, Sulawesi to Halmahera, Sumatra, Java and islands east to Tanimbar.

Bukit Teraja, Brunei (HP)

Brown Pansy ■ *Junonia hedonia* (Linnaeus, 1764)
(Borneo race – *ida*) [Brown Soldier]

HABITAT Lowlands, scrub, forest edge, shore, islands.   **ABUNDANCE** Common.

DESCRIPTION Sexes similar. Overall reddish-brown with submarginal row of small brown eyespots on hindwing. Underside greyer, with contrasting orange-brown eyespots and hazy areas of luminescent lilac scaling. Strongly indented forewing and squared apex.

SIMILAR SPECIES The less common Chocolate Pansy (opposite) is darker brown with two broad, indistinct paler bands on the wings, has less obvious eyespots on the hindwing and prefers less open habitats.

Tabin (CP)

HABITAT AND HABITS Lowlands, including open scrubland to forest edge, shore and islands. Prefers sunlit open spaces from roadside verges to fields. Often seen resting on a prominent leaf with wings open flat. When settled with wings closed resembles a dried dead leaf. Flies low with a strong, gliding flight. Feeds on flowers and rotting fruits.

LARVAL FOOD PLANT Acanthaceae (acanthus family).

RANGE Malay Peninsula (southern tip), Singapore, Borneo, Palawan, the Philippines, Sulawesi to New Guinea, Sumatra, Java to Flores, and south to N Australia.

Karambunai (HP)

In Borneo and throughout the Sunda Islands *Junonia hedonia* (the Brown Pansy) and *J. iphita* (the Chocolate Pansy) occur together (are sympatric). But in the Malay Peninsula their ranges do not overlap – *J. hedonia* is found only in the most southern state of Johore and in Singapore, whereas *J. iphita* is found only to the north of Johore.

Chocolate Pansy ■ *Junonia iphita* (Cramer, 1779)
(Borneo race – *viridis*) [Chocolate Soldier]

HABITAT Lowland to highland, forest edge.   **ABUNDANCE** Moderately common.

DESCRIPTION
Sexes similar. Dark chocolate-brown above with two broad, indistinct paler grey-brown bands following the contour of the wings. String of tiny, barely visible eyespots form a submarginal border. Underside markings as overwing but more subdued. Forewing apex square cut.

Sepilok (HP)

SIMILAR SPECIES
Darker than the more common similarly sized Brown Pansy (opposite), which is a lighter reddish-brown, more uniform in colour with more prominent eyespots, both above and below, and tends to frequent more open, sunnier habitats.

HABITAT AND HABITS Primarily lowland in open habitat within and around forest. Prefers sheltered undergrowth in partially sunlit places at the forest edge, where it feeds on wild flowers. Sometimes perches in full sunlight. Flies low down at ground level to 1m height. If disturbed flies off with a drifting, gliding flight, often settling again nearby with wings spread on low vegetation or on the leaf litter. Male is territorial.

LARVAL FOOD PLANT Urticaceae (nettle and Ramie Fibre family); Acanthaceae (acanthus family), including *Strobilanthes*, *Hygrophila* and *Justica*.

RANGE India, Sri Lanka, Myanmar, S China, Hong Kong to Taiwan, south to Malay Peninsula, Sumatra, Java, Borneo, Palawan and islands east to Sumba.

Samboja, Kalimantan (HP)

Blue Pansy ■ *Junonia orithya* (Linnaeus, 1758)
(Borneo race – *metion*)

HABITAT Grassland, shore, islands.   **ABUNDANCE** Common.

♂ *Tg Aru (CP)*

DESCRIPTION Sexes differ. Male upperside has black forewing with an irregular cream band across the wing-tip. Hindwing mostly bright blue with a cream border. Each wing has two orange and black eyespots that may be small or obscured. Female brown with similar cream markings and larger orange-ringed eyespots. Underside cryptically patterned with irregular patches in rust on pale greyish-brown.

SIMILAR SPECIES Female can be confused with the less common Peacock Pansy, which, however, has orange ground colour and larger, more dramatic hindwing eyespots.

HABITAT AND HABITS Common butterfly of grassy, open spaces in the lowlands, including parks, gardens, roadside verges, fields, coastal scrub and wasteland. Flies rapidly under the strong sun, usually about a metre above the ground. Feeds on nectar. Basks on low vegetation or on an open patch of ground. Male more often seen than female.

LARVAL FOOD PLANT Acanthaceae (acanthus family) and Scrophulariaceae (figwort and wightia family), particularly *Striga*, a tiny semi-parasite of short-cropped grass roots. The small plant is quickly devoured, the larvae frequently having to move on to a fresh plant, which often involves a wide search.

RANGE Sub-Saharan Africa, Arabian Peninsula, India, Sri Lanka, Myanmar, Thailand, S China, Hong Kong, to Ryukyu Islands, Taiwan, the Philippines, and south to Malay Peninsula, Singapore, Borneo, Sumatra, Java, to New Guinea, Solomon Islands and N Australia.

♀ *Kokol Ridge (CP)*

Tg Aru (CP)

Autumn Leaf ■ *Doleschallia bisaltide* (C. K. R. Felder, 1860)
(Borneo race – *borneensis*)

HABITAT Lowland to hill forest, rocky sites.   **ABUNDANCE** Not uncommon.

Temburong (HP)

DESCRIPTION Sexes similar, with female larger and brighter than male. Overwing golden-orange on forewing to reddish-orange on hindwing. Black forewing-tip traversed by an irregular bar of luminescent golden-orange. Diffuse dark edging to both wings. Underside grey-brown with scattered white flecks and areas of pale grey scaling. The cryptic colouring, with scaling looking like mildew, together with the shape of the projected hindwing-tip, in the shape of a leaf 'drip tip', give the appearance of a fallen leaf on the forest floor, resulting in the common name. Variable.

HABITAT AND HABITS Inhabits forested areas, particularly open, rocky sites, where it basks with wings spread under the full sun. At other times rests on undersides of leaves or in other dark places with wings closed, benefiting from its camouflaged underwing colouring to remain hidden. Swift in flight. The male employs territorial behaviour in the tree canopy, often occupying the top of a tall tree, commanding an open view, for example along a stream.

LARVAL FOOD PLANT Acanthaceae (acanthus family); elsewhere also recorded on Moraceae (fig and mulberry family), including the Jackfruit *Artocarpus heterophyllus*.

RANGE India to S China, south to Malay Peninsula, Sumatra, Java, Borneo, Palawan, the Philippines, and east through the archipelago to the Bismarcks and NE Australia.

Great Oak Leaf ■ *Kallima limborgii* (Moore, 1879)
(Borneo race – *boxtoni*) [Malayan Oak Leaf]

HABITAT Hill forest.   **ABUNDANCE** Uncommon.

DESCRIPTION Sexes similar, with female slightly larger and
paler than male. Very large and entirely distinctive. Brilliant
iridescent blue above, darkening to black at forewing apex,
contrasting with broad orange band traversing forewing.
Single white dot towards forewing apex and another just
below orange band. Underneath mottled mid-grey-brown
traversed by thin raised line. Forewing apex slightly pointed
and hindwing-tip projected. Together, shape and colouring
create the perfect resemblance to a dead leaf from which the
common name derives.

Illustration of overwing

HABITAT AND HABITS Inhabits dense forest. Typically seen in clearings or at the forest
edge. The male holds a territory and can be seen perched in a prominent position with
wings open, usually in full sunshine. If disturbed flies fast to nearby cover, where it perches
head down with wings closed on a tree trunk or among dead leaves. Here, the camouflaged
underside makes it nearly impossible to detect (see Wallace's description, in *The Malay
Archipelago*). Attracted to overripe fruits.

LARVAL FOOD PLANT Acanthaceae (acanthus family); recorded on *Strobilanthes*

callosus and
*Psuederanthemum
malabaricum* in
Malay Peninsula.
RANGE
S Myanmar,
S Thailand, to
Malay Peninsula,
Sumatra and
Borneo. Note that
about 10 species of
often very similar-
looking *Kallima* (oak
leaf butterflies) are
found from India
to central China
and southwards to
Java, with only one
species in Borneo.

Poring enclosure (CP)

Domed Sunbeam ■ *Curetis tagalica* (Felder & Felder, 1862)
(Borneo race – *jopa*)

HABITAT Lowlands to hills, forest edge.   **ABUNDANCE** Local, not common.

DESCRIPTION Sexes differ. Male above vibrant reddish-orange with a black border to the forewing, broader at the apex. Entirely luminescent white underneath, with a row of very faint grey crescents. Black-and-white banded legs. Female above has more extensive dark borders with only a central panel of tawny-orange to both wings.

SIMILAR SPECIES The most common of eight species of *Curetis* that occur in Borneo. *C. tagalica* has the most extensive orange.

HABITAT AND HABITS

Tabin (HP)

Seen at the forest edge, from the lowlands to the hills. Flies actively in strong sunshine at a height of about 1–1.5m. Typically settles with wings back, displaying white underside. However, if sunning on a leaf rests with wings half open, revealing orange upper-wing surface. Not known to visit flowers, but recorded at damp patches, on animal droppings and feeding at damaged leaf tissue.

LARVAL FOOD PLANT Leguminosae (pea, bean and mimosa family).

RANGE Borneo, Malay Peninsula, Sumatra, Java, Bali, Palawan, the Philippines and Sulawesi.

Tabin (HP)

Blue Lined Harlequin ■ *Paralaxita orphna* (Boisduval, 1836)
(Borneo race – *orphna*) [Banded Red Harlequin]

HABITAT Forest, lowland to hills.   **ABUNDANCE** Local.

Danum (CP)

DESCRIPTION Sexes differ. Underwing of both sexes brilliant red patterned with iridescent metallic blue and black radiating out from wing-base in a series of streaks and spots. Male above blackish-brown with a broad bluish-white band across the forewing and a reddened apex. Female more orange than red in ground colour, and lacks white band above.

SIMILAR SPECIES The Blue Lined Harlequin is the most common of four similar species and has both wings very rounded. White band above in male distinctive. *P. damajanti* has more pointed forewing and male above is all dark except for forewing-tip. *P. telesia* has a small 'tail', forewing more pointed and male above has small, white, oval patch, not band. *P. nicevillei* is more orange than red.

HABITAT AND HABITS Found in the shade of the forest. Typically seen perched on a flat leaf in low vegetation with wings back, displaying bright underwing. Generally sedentary, but occasionally runs forwards along a leaf, then stops abruptly, spins round and runs back. Hops about and twists and turns in short, jerky movements. If disturbed will fly off but never far, and usually settles close by on another leaf at similar height.

LARVAL FOOD PLANT Not recorded.

RANGE Myanmar, Thailand, Malay Peninsula, Borneo and Sumatra.

THE HARLEQUIN & THE GINGER

Most people are familiar with the name ginger in relation to the hot spicy rhizome, or root, of the plant *Zingiber officinale* used in cookery and medicine. The plant that produces this root is a member of the family Zingiberaceae, native to Southeast Asia, and is also known as a ginger. Gingers are pantropical, chiefly occurring in Indo-Malaysia, which hosts about 80 per cent of all known species. Nearly 250 ginger species occur in Borneo. Gingers grow wild in tropical forests, especially in the lowlands, and particularly along rivers. Some species also rapidly colonize disturbed areas such as along the edges of access roads.

Globba atrosanguinea, Mulu forest (HP)

Gingers are herbaceous plants 20cm–8m tall, depending on the species, usually with multiple arching stems, relatively large, oval, often crinkly leaves, in opposite rows, and generally bright, showy flowers that emerge from a cluster of bracts. In the understorey of the forest many of them are pollinated by bees. However, there is one group of gingers that utilizes a butterfly for pollination. Gingers in the genus known as *Globbas* have an elongated, arching filament/style. It

is believed that the Harlequin butterfly, *P. orphna*, pollinates gingers in this genus, such as *Globba atrosanguinea*, illustrated, which grows low down in the shade of the forest (Anthony Lamb, personal observation). When the butterfly lands on the flower to sip nectar, its wing-tips brush against the anthers, collecting pollen, which is then transferred to the receptive stigma on a flower it visits subsequently, thus effecting pollination.

This is just one example of the countless and complex relationships between plants and animals in the rainforest.

Illustration of Harlequin visiting ginger

Banded Blue Pierrot ■ *Discolampa ethion* (Westwood, 1851)
(Borneo race – *icenus*)

HABITAT Lowland forest, along streams.   **ABUNDANCE** Local, not uncommon.

DESCRIPTION Sexes differ. Male underneath, illustrated, has well-defined black markings, including two basal stripes, on a white background. Female similar but with slimmer black markings. Male above has wide black border to both wings and inner to that strong blue – glimpsed in flight – and white central panel. Female above similar but without any blue. Short, filamentous tail in both sexes.

SIMILAR SPECIES Could be confused with the Elbowed Pierrot (opposite) of similar habitat, but that species is larger, and has fewer and heavier black markings.

HABITAT AND HABITS Found in the vicinity of streams or rivers in lowland primary forest. Flight low and swift. Males settle on damp ground to sip water. Viewed from a distance, scattered black markings on a white background of wing pattern break up the shape of the butterfly, making it hard to see on a pebble-strewn riverbank – a protective adaptation known as disruptive colouration (p. 20). In close proximity the same black and white pattern may also serve as a warning.

LARVAL FOOD PLANT Not yet recorded in Borneo. Elsewhere reported on Rhamnaceae (jujube and buckthorn family); on *Zizyphus jujuba* in India and Java.

RANGE India, Sri Lanka, Myanmar, to S China, Hainan, and south through Thailand, Malay Peninsula, Sumatra, Java, Bali, Borneo, Palawan, the Philippines, and Sulawesi to Flores.

Tabin (HP)

Elbowed Pierrot ■ *Caleta elna* (Hewitson, 1876)
(Borneo race – *elvira*)

HABITAT Lowland to hill forest, near streams and rivers. **ABUNDANCE** Locally common.

Poring (CP)

DESCRIPTION Sexes similar. Underside white with heavy black markings with blurred edges like ink on damp paper. Prominent wide black basal band forming distinct right angle runs from forewing to hindwing, giving rise to the common name. Then an irregular row of large, conjoined spots and an intricate black margin. Upperside black with broad white central panel to forewing and hindwing. Short, black, white-tipped, thread-like tail. Colouring cryptic from a distance against dappled background, but at close proximity black and white colouration acts as a warning (see p. 20).

SIMILAR SPECIES In the Bornean Straight Pierrot *C. manovus* prominent basal black band on underwing is narrower and smoothly curved instead of sharply angled.

HABITAT AND HABITS Flutters close to the ground in dappled shade at the forest edge. Comes to damp ground to take moisture. Settles to drink or feed with wings back, displaying the underwing. Occasionally basks in the sun on a stone or on a low leaf with wings partially open. Visits flowers for nectar. May be encountered at the same spot several days running. Sometimes congregates with other species. Visits damp ash for the uptake of trace elements.

LARVAL FOOD PLANT Rhamnaceae (buckthorn and jujube family).

RANGE N India, Nepal, Bhutan, Myanmar, Thailand, Malay Peninsula, Singapore, Sumatra, Java, Borneo, Palawan and Sulawesi.

Poring (CP)

Cycad Blue ■ *Chilades pandava* (Horsfield, 1829)
[Plains Cupid]

HABITAT Seashore and islands, parks, gardens.

ABUNDANCE Locally common.

Tanjung Aru (QP)

DESCRIPTION Sexes differ. Settles with wings back and underwing showing. Underside of both sexes pale grey-brown with a series of broken, wavy pale lines following wing contour. Short, white-tipped filamentous tail. Also, large black, orange-crowned spot alongside two smaller spots by base of tail. Male above mid-purplish-blue, except for a narrow dark border and a single black spot by the tail. Female paler blue, with a broad dark border on forewing and submarginal spots on hindwing.

SIMILAR SPECIES *C. mindora* is also seen on cycads but is less common, occurs singly, and underneath is pale instead of grey-brown, with rows of black spots instead of pale lines.

HABITAT AND HABITS Found along the seashore among strand vegetation or in gardens or parks, settled on or flying around the cycad food plant in full sun. Gregarious and tends to occur in small groups, gathering on one plant in large numbers even when there are other cycads available nearby. Eggs laid singly or in small batches of up to 10 on new shoots. Larvae attended by several ant species.

LARVAL FOOD PLANT Cycadaceae, especially *Cycas revoluta* (ornamental sago palm), and *C. circinalis*.

RANGE India, Myanmar, Thailand, China, Hainan, Hong Kong, Taiwan, Malay Peninsula, Singapore, Sumatra, Java, Bali, Borneo, Palawan, the Philippines, and many intervening islands, including Andamans, Nicobars and Langkawi.

Sepilok (CP)

THE CYCAD BLUE AND ITS HOST PLANT, THE CYCAD (CYCADACEAE)

Cycads are ancient plants that date from the time of the dinosaurs. They have a stout, woody trunk with a crown of large, tough, usually pinnate, evergreen leaves and are often mistaken for small palms (Arecaceae). Cycads are very slow growing and long lived.

It is not unusual to see a small cloud of Cycad Blues fluttering around the crown of a single cycad plant preparing to lay their eggs. The butterfly lays its eggs on the tender young shoots at the centre of the plant. Once the eggs hatch, the tiny larvae burrow into the centre of the new leaf and begin to eat the pith. Because of the large number of larvae involved, very soon the leaves on which they are feeding begin to wither and die. The larvae usually decimate the host plant by destroying the new growth, leaving only old leaves in an outer ring. However, despite the considerable damage done, the cycad plant survives defoliation, as once an individual plant has died back at the centre, the butterflies leave it to colonize another plant, allowing the host plant to regenerate over time. Cycads are extremely hardy as they store energy in the form of starch in their trunks. Many other plants would not be able to recover from this amount of damage. Furthermore, native cycads, *Cycas litoralis*, are still relatively abundant in Borneo, both along the shore of the mainland and on offshore islands, so that only a small proportion of the cycad plant population is colonized by the butterflies at any point in time, while the remainder of the plants are free to thrive, and to set seed and produce further new plants.

A large quantity of eggs is laid by the gregarious butterflies – visible here as the small dots in neat rows on the new leaves at the centre of the picture, Karambunai (CP)

Ciliate Blue ■ *Anthene emolus* (Godart, 1824)

(Borneo race – *goberus*)

HABITAT Forest to farmland.   **ABUNDANCE** Moderately common.

DESCRIPTION Sexes differ. Male above entirely shining violet-blue, except a thin black edging to both wings. Female brown with pale blue at wing-base. Hindwing fringed with tiny hairs (cilia). Underside mid-greyish-brown traversed by thin, pale wavy lines. Hindwing has a prominent orange-crowned black eyespot on outer margin and a distinct black spot midway on lower margin. No tails, but three short, tail-like tufts.

SIMILAR SPECIES The less common Pointed Ciliate Blue *A. lycaenina* has a more angular shape to wings and more numerous and paler lines underneath.

HABITAT AND HABITS Found at damp patches on forest roads or among low vegetation at the forest fringe, especially near streams; also in secondary growth in open country. Flies in the open under the direct sun. Attracted to human sweat and habitually settles on people to take moisture from bare skin or even through clothing.

LARVAL FOOD PLANT No records for Borneo. Elsewhere on a variety of plants, including Leguminosae (bean family); *Cassia fistula, Saraca thaipingensis* in Malay Peninsula.

Larvae attended by Kerengga (weaver ants) *Oecophylla smaragdina*.

RANGE From India, east to S China, the Philippines, Palawan, and south through Malay Peninsula, Singapore, Borneo, Sumatra, Java and Bali, east to Sumbawa.

Kimanis (HP)

Kerengga Ant

Kadazan Lass ■ *Heliophorus kiana* (Grose-Smith, 1889) ⓔ

HABITAT High montane. **ABUNDANCE** Local, not uncommon.

♀ *Kinabalu Park HQ (HP)*

DESCRIPTION Sexes differ. Both golden-yellow underneath, with a red-orange margin. Hindwing margin contains a row of black spots in a white patch. Forewing fringed with dark hairs and hindwing with white hairs; short, corkscrew, feathery white tail that flutters in the wind. Both sexes dark purple-brown above. Male has iridescent pale blue patch at end of hindwing, containing single dark spot. Female has bluish-white patch with a faint row of dark spots, one bolder than the others.

HABITAT AND HABITS So far known only from Mt Kinabalu and the Crocker Range in Sabah, north Borneo. Found along mountain ridges, this small, beautiful butterfly manages to thrive in the often cold, wet and windy conditions on mountains. Flies low and swiftly, sometimes perching on vegetation in the sunshine in more open areas, such as by streams or along paths. Visits flowers for nectar and damp ground to drink.

LARVAL FOOD PLANT Polygonaceae (buckwheat and dock family); *Polygonum chinense* – preferring plants growing in dark places in the forest.

RANGE Endemic to Borneo. Discovered by Whitehead on his expedition to Mt Kinabalu in 1888 (p. 123). Generic name derived from the Greek *helio*, meaning sun and *-phoros*, meaning bearing or carrying, while *kiana* means from or pertaining to Kiau, the locality on Mount Kinabalu.

♀ *Kinabalu Park HQ (QP)*

Oak blues ■ *Arhopala* spp. (Boisduval, 1832)

HABITAT Predominantly lowland primary forest.

ABUNDANCE Not uncommon.

Eighty-nine species of the *Arhopala* genus have been recorded in Borneo and most of them look dauntingly alike. They are covered in detail by Otsuka et al., *Butterflies of Borneo* (1991). This overview entry is only intended to enable identification to genus level.

DESCRIPTION In *The Butterflies of the Malay Peninsula* (1934), Corbet and Pendlebury wrote, 'Normally, both sexes are shining blue or purple above, with narrow black borders in the male and broader borders in the female … Usually the underside is

Mulu (HP)

hair brown, with darker rounded spots in the basal half of each wing … Most of the species have a filamentous tail …' Most have one or more black spots set amid iridescent pale blue scaling at the hindwing-tip.

HABITAT AND HABITS Generally found in lowland primary forest, although *A. centaurus* also occurs in secondary growth and gardens, and six species in Borneo occur only at high elevations. 'They are rather unobtrusive in habit, do not visit flowers, and spend much time settled on the leaves of shrubs and bushes some 4 to 10 feet from the ground, whence they make only occasional short flights. When the sun goes in they often leave these lowly perches and fly up into the forest canopy.' (Corbet and Pendlebury).

Kota Kinabalu area (CP)

LARVAL FOOD PLANT The known larval food plants are predominantly Fagaceae (oak, beech and chestnut family). Larvae of many species are attended by ants.

RANGE India, Sri Lanka east to S China, Japan, and south through the Philippines, Malay Peninsula, Sumatra, Java, Borneo, east to the Solomon Islands, and south to N Australia.

Pale-tailed Yamfly ■ *Loxura cassiopeia* (Distant, 1884)
(Borneo race – *amatica*) [Malayan Yamfly]

HABITAT Lowland to hills, forest edge.   **ABUNDANCE** Not common.

DESCRIPTION Sexes differ. Underside entirely apricot-orange with faint darker markings forming chain pattern across both wings. Female slightly paler than male. On upperside, male is bright reddish-orange with a black border to the forewing, wider at the apex, and dark dusted wing-bases. Female darker, with most of the orange wing expanse dusted brown. Hindwing extended at tip to form a long white ribbon tail with a twist. Hindwing lightly fringed with short white hairs (cilia).

SIMILAR SPECIES Distinguished from the more common *L. atymnus* by larger size, forewing border above extending along leading wing edge (costa) to base of wing, lack of black spot at base of tail and all-pale tail.

HABITAT AND HABITS Flies in the sunshine at the forest edge. Flies restlessly and speedily among bushes and shrubbery at about 2m height. Occasionally settles for a while in full sunshine on a low leaf. Habitually settles with wings folded back in upright position.

LARVAL FOOD PLANT Dioscoreaceae (yam family), *Dioscora*.

RANGE Malay Peninsula, Sumatra, Borneo, Palawan and Mindanao (the Philippines).

Poring (CP)

Chocolate Royal ■ *Remelana jangala* (Horsfield, 1829)
(Borneo race – *huberta*)

HABITAT Lowland to hill forest.   **ABUNDANCE** Moderately common.

Sungai Wain (HP)

DESCRIPTION Sexes broadly similar. Underside uniformly mid-brown with thread-like, dark brown line across both wings. Two prominent black spots at hindwing-tip set in metallic blue-green scaling. Two white-tipped black, filamentous tails of medium length. Dark chocolate-brown above, shot with deep lustrous purple in basal half of both wings. Female similar to male but paler, with more extensive purple on over-wing.

HABITAT AND HABITS Found in forested areas from lowlands to hills. Stays low, settling on low bushes or the forest floor. Short, rapid flight. Occasionally visits damp ground. When settled on a flat surface it can flex its wings so that the eyespots are displayed horizontally, creating a very effective false head illusion (see p. 22).

LARVAL FOOD PLANT Not recorded in Borneo. Recorded on Araliaceae (ivy and ginseng family) in Celebes; on Ericaceae (*Rhododendron* spp.) and Guttiferae (mangosteen family) in Hong Kong; also on *Rhododendron* spp. in India. Larvae attended by ants.

RANGE N India east to S China, Hong Kong, the Philippines, south through Malay Peninsula, Singapore, Borneo, Palawan, Sulawesi, Sumatra and Java, and east to Flores.

Yellow Banded Awl ■ *Hasora schoenherr* (Latreille, 1824)
(Borneo race – *chuza*)

HABITAT Lowland to hill primary forest.　　　**ABUNDANCE** Not uncommon.

DESCRIPTION
Sexes similar. Ground colour dark brown, but paler tawny-brown beneath, especially at wing-bases. Hindwing has a broad yellow transverse band central to wing that is distinctive. Forewing has three large, pale spots mid-wing forming disjointed band, and four small, pale spots in a row towards apex. Forewing slender and pointed. Hindwing

Temburong (CP)

lobed. Forewing fringed with tiny brown hairs (cilia) and hindwing with yellow ones. Antennae pale but dark tipped.

HABITAT AND HABITS Found at the edge of lowland or hill forest, and favours open but lightly shaded areas. Mostly seen singly. Active early in the day and at dusk (crepuscular). Flight swift. Settles with wings upright. Sometimes rests on underside of a leaf, where it is hidden from view. Occasionally seen near buildings at the forest edge.

LARVAL FOOD PLANT Not recorded in Borneo. On Leguminosae (beans, peas and mimosa family) in Malay Peninsula (on *Fordia ngii*) and Palawan (on *Spatholobus palawanensis*).

RANGE Myanmar and Thailand, to Vietnam, south to Malay Peninsula, Singapore (very rare), Sumatra, Java, Borneo, Palawan and the Philippines.

One of a group known as 'pied flats' ■ *Coladenia palawana*
(Staudinger, 1889; no subspecies described)

HABITAT Forest, all elevations.   **ABUNDANCE** Not recorded.

DESCRIPTION Sexes broadly similar. Overall an iridescent, pink-tinged copper-brown, with female paler than male. Forewing has four large, translucent spots in a loose band mid-wing and three small spots (five in female) outer to that. Hindwing has two rows of faint, smudgy dark spots. Hindwing has distinctive indentation on outer edge.
SIMILAR SPECIES *C. agni* has four small spots at apex of forewing, and *Psuedocoladenia dan* is more rufous; both have hindwing typically rounded, not squared.
HABITAT AND HABITS Found at forest edge including along pathways. Often perches on a low, broad prominent leaf in bright sunshine. Typically rests with wings held flat but sometimes with forewings raised at a 45-degree angle.
LARVAL FOOD PLANT Not recorded in Borneo. On *Allophylus cobbe*, Sapindaceae (rambutan, lychee and maple family) in Malay Peninsula.
RANGE Malay Peninsula, Sumatra, Bali, Borneo and Palawan (but absent from Java).

Poring (CP)

Common Snow Flat ■ *Tagiades japetus* (Stoll, 1781)
(Borneo race – *balana*)

HABITAT Lowlands to hills, forest edge.   **ABUNDANCE** Moderately common.

Poring (HP)

DESCRIPTION Sexes similar. All brown above; darker towards wing edge and darker smudges across mid-wings. Three small white spots in a row near forewing apex and a further one, sometimes two, inner to that. Forewing brown underneath as above, but hindwing has a partial pale blue-white wash. Female larger than male.

SIMILAR SPECIES The most common of nine similar species distinguished by the complete absence of any white on upper surface of hindwing, present in all the other species.

HABITAT AND HABITS Found at the margin of both primary and secondary forest, favouring full sunshine. Most active in the early morning. Flight swift. Settles with wings fully outspread, landing either on or under leaves, often on taller shrubs or trees. Comes down for nectar from wayside flowers such as the common 'snakeweed' featured in the photos (see also p. 170).

LARVAL FOOD PLANT Dioscoreaceae (yam family), Convolvulaceae (bindweed, sweet potato and kangkong family).

RANGE From India, Sri Lanka, east to Hainan, the Philippines, Palawan, south to Malay Peninsula, Singapore, Borneo, Sulawesi, Sumatra, Java, east to New Guinea, Solomon Islands, and south to NE Australia.

Glimpse of underside with pale hindwing (CP)

Monster Skipper ■ *Odontoptilum pygela* (Hewitson, 1868)
(Borneo race – *pygela*) [Banded Angle]

HABITAT Forest, lowland to hills, islands.   **ABUNDANCE** Not common.

Belalong (CP)

DESCRIPTION Sexes similar. Dark reddish-brown above, with extensive white area towards hindwing-tip and white fringing to hindwing. Stout appearance. Note sharply stepped outline to hindwing (resulting in the name Banded Angle in W Malaysia). Underside has all brown forewing; hindwing almost entirely white. Female slightly more rufous-brown than male, and with thick hair tuft on tip of abdomen. Tip of each antenna (the apiculus) is blunt and not tapered to a fine point.

HABITAT AND HABITS Occurs along riverbanks and in other open spaces in forested areas from the lowlands to the hills. Flies under the full sun. Visits damp ground to take up mineral-rich water. Occurs singly but sometimes joins a mixed-species puddling group. Settles with wings spread flat. Male often rests on leaves or rocks. On rocks it is well camouflaged due to both colouring and posture. Also visits flowers. Female rarely seen.

LARVAL FOOD PLANT Unrecorded.

RANGE S Myanmar, S Thailand, Malay Peninsula, Borneo, Sumatra, Java, Bangka Island, Nias Island and Palawan.

Black and White Flat ■ *Gerosis limax* (Plotz, 1884)
(Borneo race – *dirae*)

HABITAT Lowland to hill primary forest.   **ABUNDANCE** Not recorded.

DESCRIPTION Sexes broadly similar. Wings copper-brown overall, with some darker smudges. Hindwing outline somewhat angular. Large, white, more or less round, blurry edged patch mid-hindwing in male distinctive. Hindwing white area more extensive in female, covering most of wing surface. Three medium and five smaller translucent spots on forewing in both sexes.

SIMILAR SPECIES For male, none. Female similar to closely related but slightly smaller *G. sinica*.

HABITAT AND HABITS Inhabits lowland forest and might be seen along any wide, shady footpath. Typically perches with wings flat on a broad, low leaf in a patch of sunshine. Active in the daytime. Flight fast. Rare through most of its range.

LARVAL FOOD PLANT Recorded on *Abrus precatorius*, Leguminosae (bean, pea and mimosa family) in Malay Peninsula.

RANGE S Myanmar, S Thailand, Malay Peninsula, Singapore (very rare), Sumatra, Java, Bali, Borneo and Palawan.

Danum (CP)

Bright Red Velvet Bob ■ *Koruthaialos sindu* (C&R Felder, 1860)

HABITAT Edge of forest, lowland to hills.   **ABUNDANCE** Common.

DESCRIPTION Sexes similar. Dark brown with prominent broad, orange-red band across forewing. Band somewhat variable in width, and paler and broader in female than male. Settles with wings held at 45-degree angle above the body.

SIMILAR SPECIES In the same genus, *K. rubecula* is very similar but red band is narrower and shorter and does not extend to wing edge. *K. frena* is larger, with a wider, more orange band and only occurs in the highlands of Mt Kinabalu.

HABITAT AND HABITS Frequents sunlit vegetation at the forest margin. Most often found at any time of day resting on the surface of a large, prominent leaf of a bush in full sunshine. If disturbed usually returns to the same spot or nearby.

LARVAL FOOD PLANT Zingiberaceae (ginger family) and Musaceae (banana family).

RANGE India to Malay Peninsula, Sumatra, Java, Bali, Borneo and Palawan.

Sepilok (CP)

Banded Demon   *Notocrypta paralysos* (Wood-Mason & de Niceville, 1881)
(Borneo race – *varians*)

HABITAT Edge of forest, lowland to hills.   **ABUNDANCE** Common.

Mesilau, Kinabalu (CP)

DESCRIPTION Sexes similar. Entirely black both above and below, appearing more dark brown in bright sunlight. Underside has purple-brown tinge. Prominent, irregular white transverse band mid-forewing. Single white dot outer to white band may be present (more often in females than in males) or absent.

SIMILAR SPECIES The most common of six species of *Notocrypta* in Borneo. Most similar are *N. clavata* and *N. pria*. Both have a thinner white band. *N. clavata* larger and has no white spot. *N. pria* smaller and rarer, and mostly found in open country.

HABITAT AND HABITS Found in primary or secondary forests in clearings or along forest paths from the lowland to the hills. Flies fast at around 0.5–1.5m high. Spends much time settled on any prominent large leaf of low vegetation in full sunshine. Rests with hindwings flat and forewings up at 45 degrees. Often returns to the same perching spot if disturbed. Visits wayside flowers such as Snakeweed (*Stachytarpheta indica*) for nectar.

LARVAL FOOD PLANT Zingiberaceae (ginger family).

RANGE India, Sri Lanka, to S China, south to Malay Peninsula, Singapore, Sumatra, Java, Borneo, the Philippines, Sulawesi and islands of the archipelago.

Kimanis (HP)

One of a group commonly known as 'lancers' ■
Pyroneura spp. (Eliot, 1978)

HABITAT Forest understorey, forest edge.   **ABUNDANCE** Most species rare, or very rare, but a few are moderately abundant.

Sungai Wain (HP)

DESCRIPTION Previously classified as *Plastingia*. Nine species occur in Borneo, many of which are indistinguishable in the field. Some of the most brightly coloured and intricately patterned of all the skippers. Veins on underside narrowly to broadly dusted in yellow, orange or red. Spaces between are black with white and blue angular spots and streaks. Typically dark brown above, splashed with yellow or orange streaks and translucent spots. Both wings fringed with tiny hairs (cilia) coloured orange to brown. In males upper forelegs furred with yellow hairs. In some species antennae are partly yellow, usually the club or apiculus (hooked tip).

HABITAT AND HABITS The butterflies fly in shaded parts of the forest understorey or forest edge, and typically rest on the upper surface of a leaf with wings closed upright. Flight fast. They visit flowers. Generally active by day but sometimes also at dusk. The majority of species are found in lowland to hill primary forest. Exceptionally, *P. aurantiaca* is a highland to montane species found above 750m. *P. niasana* can be found at any elevation. *P. latoia* sometimes found in secondary forest.

LARVAL FOOD PLANT Not recorded, but most likely on Palmae (palms).

RANGE Mainly confined to Malay Peninsula, Sumatra, Java, Borneo and Palawan (but some species extend to southern Myanmar, one to N India and one to the Philippines).

Wild Silk Moth ■ *Antheraea platessa (jana)* (Rothschild)

DESCRIPTION Saturniidae are found worldwide and this family includes some of the largest and most decorative and spectacular moths in the world. 'The general aspect of these moths is of enormous wings, often with "eyes" or transparent "windows", attached to short hairy stubby bodies. The adult moths have short antennae, complex in both sexes, small heads and large eyes.' (A. Fox, 1986). Antennae are comb-like (pectinate). The proboscis is insignificant or absent. Females are larger than the males. The forewing in the male is more curved (falcate).

'The newly-emerged females, heavy with eggs, often remain still after the wings have developed, sending out sexual signals for males in the area.' Avril Fox, *Common Malaysian Moths*, 1986. The larvae pupate in a silken cocoon, which 'is wrapped in leaf fragments and suspended by a short stalk from a twig' (J. D. Holloway, *The Moths of Borneo*, 1987). The coarse silk of some species is used commercially in parts of India.

HABITAT Rare inhabitant of lowland rainforest.

RANGE Myanmar to S China, and south to Malay Peninsula, Sumatra, Java and Borneo.

♀ *Danum (HP)*

THE TRUE SILK MOTH
Bombyx mori in the closely related Bombycidae family is the infamous true 'silk moth'. 'All the fine silk in the world has been spun by the larvae of this moth … because of one unique feature: the caterpillars spin an unbroken strand of silk when they make their cocoons which can extend to 3000 yards in length.' (A. Fox, 1986) It takes approximately 3,000 cocoons to make one pound of silk.

Tiger Moth ▪ *Areas galactina* (Hoeven)

Rose Cabin, near Kinabalu Park HQ (CP)

The Erebidae is a worldwide family and variations of 'tiger moth' are found on every continent. They are distinguished by the striking combination of the boldly patterned, black and white forewings and the bright red, orange or yellow hindwings and body. They are a good example of aposematic or warning colouration (p. 20). The larvae feed on plants containing toxins, including wild figs, which make them repellent to potential predators such as birds. Note also the fine black antennae with a white section towards the tip.

The wings of these moths are held over the body when at rest, but if disturbed the forewings are flicked open, flashing the bright orange hindwings and red body to startle and warn off any potential predator.

HABITAT An uncommon montane species so far recorded in Mt Kinabalu, Sabah and Mt Api (Mulu Park) and Penrissen, Sarawak.

RANGE N India to SW China, Taiwan, Malay Peninsula, Sumatra, Java, Borneo and the Philippines.

INSECTIVOROUS BATS
Insectivorous bats consume thousands of night-flying moths. The bats navigate and hunt by using ultrasonic sound emissions by which means they locate their prey on the wing. Some species in the Erebidae moth family are able to produce a high-frequency sound that can be used to confuse or repel bats and thus avoid being eaten.

Dead Leaf Moth ■ *Phyllodes eyndhovii* (Vollenhoven)

DESCRIPTION One of a large and varied subfamily of medium to large moths, most of which have brown-patterned wings. They have well-developed proboscies that can be used to pierce fruit skins so as to feed on the juice. In this genus, forewings have a distinctive leaf shape and subtle and complex colouring, including an apparent leaf mid-rib and a blotch resembling mildew or decay, which result in perfect leaf mimicry. The generic name comes from the Greek *phyllo*, meaning leaf. When at rest with the forewings held over the body, *P. eyndhovii* is well camouflaged, resembling dead leaves. However, if disturbed, it displays the bright orange and black hindwings to startle and deter a potential predator (see also p. 23). The Dead Leaf Moth has been recorded piercing fruits in Thailand.

HABITAT Recorded in cultivation adjacent to forest, from lowlands (among orchards at Sepilok), to lower montane habitat (Kundasan, Mt Kinabalu).

LARVAL FOOD PLANT The principal larval host plant family of the *Phyllodes* is Menispermaceae (chiefly lianas of tropical lowland rainforest), but Dead Leaf Moth larvae have been recorded on *Acacia* (Leguminosae) in Thailand.

RANGE N India, W China, Taiwan, Thailand, Malay Peninsula, Borneo, Sumatra, Java and Palawan.

Sepilok (HP)

■ *Asota kinabaluensis* (Rothschild, 1896)

Mt Kinabalu, near Park HQ Buildings, 1,500m (CP)

The bold, patchy black and white wing pattern is distinctive. The abdomen, not visible when at rest, is yellow ringed with black. This is warning colouration indicative of the larvae feeding on toxic plants, and it is known that the majority of species in this genus feed on *Ficus* (Moraceae, fig family), and build up nauseating substances in their bodies, which deter potential predators (p. 22). The slender, tapering antennae are 'finely feathered' with small, closely set projections like the teeth of a comb. The moths in this family rest with their wings held over the body in the shape of a tent.

HABITAT Montane but most common in upper montane forest. Recorded in Mt Kinabalu, Sabah, Mt Mulu, Sarawak and Bukit Retak, Brunei.

RANGE Endemic to Borneo.

WALTER ROTHSCHILD
Walter Rothschild, 1868–1937, was born into the wealthy international family banking dynasty. However, he had a strong interest in the natural world from childhood, especially in entomology and particularly butterflies. He left the family business after a few years to follow his own interests. He established a zoological museum at Tring near London and funded zoological expeditions all over the world. Many newly discovered species and subspecies were named after him. On his death he bequeathed his museum and all its contents to the British Museum (Natural History section). This remains the largest bequest the British Museum has ever received.

The Dazzler ■ *Milionia zonea* (Moore, 1872)

DESCRIPTION This brightly coloured, rather robust moth flies by day and can easily be mistaken for a butterfly. However, the electric-blue body and antennae that taper to a point distinguish it as a moth. Butterfly antennae always end in a club tip (see also p. 16), and no butterflies possess such a vividly coloured body. The iridescent blue of the body, which extends partially up the wings from the wing-base, is only clearly visible in certain lighting conditions.

The male antennae are fringed with fine hairs (ciliate). This moth also comes to light at night.

HABITAT Lowland forest to lower montane and upper montane forest.

Kinabalu National Park HQ, 1,500m (CP)

LARVAL FOOD PLANTS 'The indications are that the genus is a conifer specialist, particularly on Podocarpaceae and Araucariaceae, southern hemisphere families that extend north to eastern Asia.' (J. D. Holloway, *The Moths of Borneo*, 1987). Podocarps are a common component of montane forest higher up on Mt Kinabalu, particularly on exposed ridges and on poor soil.

RANGE NE Himalayas to Taiwan, Japan, the Philippines, Malay Peninsula, Sumatra, Java, Borneo and Palawan.

Kinabalu National Park HQ, 1,500m (CP)

White-peppered-black Moth ■ *Amblychia cavimargo* (Prout, 1925)

♀ *resting on a tree trunk by day, along a forest path, Mt Kinabalu (CP)*

DESCRIPTION Male overall rather darker and more evenly coloured than female, with a slimmer abdomen. Male antennae appear feathery, whereas those of the female appear thread-like. This is among the biggest species in the Geometridae, a numerous family varying greatly in size. Typically, in the Geometridae, the wings are large relative to the body and the moths usually rest with all four wings spread out.

'Cryptic coloration … applies to many insects … There are many moths which rest … during the day, for example on light bark that is covered with lichens. The moths sit with spread wings and the colour and patterning of the wings often resembles that of the substrate so exactly that it is virtually impossible to find them.' (Wolfgang Wickler, *Mimicry in Plants and Animals*, 1986).

'Wherever lichens are a conspicuous feature of the environment, as on tree trunks or on stone walls, a variety of insects … have a remarkably deceptive resemblance to them.'

Well camouflaged, at rest, Mt Kinabalu (CP)

'The irregular dimensional form of a lichen is mimicked not by the animal's shape but, as Cott described, by "the most ingenious and deceptive disruptive patterns, which give the optical impression of irregular processes and deep interstices – even when painted, as they often are, on the flat canvas of a moth's wing…" ' (Gilbert Waldbauer, *How Not to Be Eaten*, 2012).

HABITAT Occurs in upper montane forest. On Mt Kinabalu, frequent from Park HQ, 1,500m–1,930m. Also recorded at Mt Mulu, Sarawak and at Bukit Retak, Brunei.

RANGE Endemic to Borneo.

Broken Twig Moth ■ *Phalera sundana* (Holloway, 1982)

DESCRIPTION The Notodontidae have, as Avril Fox (*Common Malaysian Moths*) wrote, 'a remarkable talent for camouflage' both as larvae and as adult moths. When at rest with its wings furled around the body in typical notodontid fashion, *P. sundana* 'exactly resembles a silvery broken off twig'. Notodontids fly late at night and often feign death if captured. They are among the moths that possess a tympanum, or hearing organ, and are regarded as highly evolved by taxonomists. Their proboscis is non-functioning, so they cannot feed as adults and must mate quickly, afterwards dying in a few days.

HABITAT Common in lowland rainforest of most types, but most abundant in alluvial forest and kerangas; recorded at Maliau.

RANGE SE China, S Thailand, Malay Peninsula, Sumatra, Java, Bali, Borneo, Palawan and the Philippines.

Temburong River, Brunei (HP)

The Golden Imposter ■ *Callidula* spp.

Kinabalu National Park, Mesilau, 1,200m (CP)

DESCRIPTION There are seven species of Callidula moth in Borneo, mostly very similar in appearance. These moths are darker above, often with a pale subapical band across the forewing. Underneath pale golden-orange with darker striations, also usually with some silvery, dark-ringed, irregular spots. They have simple, thread-like antennae tapering to a point but note also that the tip is slightly upturned.

HABITAT AND HABITS Callidula moths are generally found in shady places along streams, flying low over the vegetation. They are primarily day-flying moths. When settled they hold their wings vertically over their backs. These two facts result in them being easily mistaken for small butterflies. However, their threadlike antennae (which are neither clubbed nor hooked) straightaway confirm their identity as moths.

LARVAL FOOD PLANTS The recorded larval food plants of the Callidula are exclusively ferns. The larvae roll individual leaflets or groups of leaflets together with silk, living and pupating within the roll.

RANGE Restricted to Southeast Asia, ranging from southern Siberia, south, and from India to the Solomons Islands.

Moth Predator

A good place to see moths is around the veranda or porch lights at night, if staying anywhere near the forest edge. However, geckos also wait there hoping to snatch a meal. This is the moment a *Lyssa menoetius* moth (one of the largest moths in Borneo, with a wingspan of 12cm) met an untimely end in the jaws of *Gekko smithii*, the Giant Green-eyed Forest Gecko, the largest gecko in Borneo (up to 35 cm long, including tail). *Gekko smithii* has a curious call, like a low, growling dog's bark, and is often heard but seldom seen.

Ulu Ulu Resort, Temburong River, Brunei (HP)

Many moths are protected from predation at the larval (caterpillar) stage by having long, stinging hairs (see below right).

Lyssa menoetius, *Temburong (HP)*   *A moth caterpillar, Mulu (HP)*

Eggs, Larvae and Pupae

Some examples of the variety of forms and colours of eggs, larvae and pupal cases of different species of butterfly.

Not to scale (except small image of egg which is lifesize).

PAPILIONIDAE Great Mormon *Papilio Memnon* (p.36)

EGG   LARVA   PUPA

Note false head

Egg size: 1.8mm

Real head

PIERIDAE Common Grass Yellow *Eurema hecabe* (p.65)

EGG   LARVA   PUPA

Suspended by silken girdle

Often lies along leaf midrib

Egg size: 1.3mm (height)

NYMPHALIDAE Dark Glassy Tiger *Parantica agleoides*

EGG   LARVA   PUPA

Egg size: 1.7mm (height)

NYMPHALIDAE Malayan Eggfly *Hypolimnas anomala* (p.128)

EGG   LARVA   PUPA

Egg size: 0.6mm (height)

NYMPHALIDAE Horsfield's Baron *Tanaecia iapis* (p. 121)

EGG   LARVA   PUPA

Egg size: 1.8mm

NYMPHALIDAE Plain Nawab *Polyura hebe*

EGG   LARVA   PUPA

Egg size: 1.5mm

LYCAENIDAE Common Posy *Drupadia ravindra*

EGG   LARVA
Lycaenidae larvae are often
attended by ants   PUPA

Egg size: 0.9mm

HESPERIIDAE Plain Banded Awl *Hasora vitta*

EGG   LARVA   PUPA
The larva lives within shelter
of leaves sewn together with its
own silk

Egg size: 0.6mm

LEGS AND CLASPERS

4 pairs of claspers ——————   L————— 3 pairs of true legs

SOME EXAMPLES OF LARVAL FOOD PLANTS

CHINESE BANYAN
Malay: Jejawi
Ficus microcarpa
Moraceae

Larval food plant of the Striped Blue Crow (p. 79) and some other related species. A common strangling fig, this is often found in town parks and coastal forests either as an epiphyte or often as a very large, stand-alone tree with multiple trunks. Can be recognised from the multiple thin, reddish brown aerial roots, which hang from the branches and which often grow down to root in the ground. The figs are pea sized and ripen white to pink to dark red. Ornamental varieties, some with yellow leaves, may be grown for landscaping or cultivated as bonsai. If damaged, all parts of the plant produce a sticky white latex to deter insect attack, however, caterpillars of the Striped Blue Crow are able to eat the leaves without ill effect.

SEVEN GOLDEN CANDLESTICKS
Malay: Gelenggang
Senna alata Leguminosae (Caesalpinioideae)
Larval food plant of the Mottled Emigrant (p. 63). A large number of the well-camouflaged eggs, larvae and pupae may be found together on one plant. Introduced from tropical America, this plant species is now common growing wild in waste places in the lowlands, especially in damp locations. It is a large, straggly shrub to 3m tall, with branches spread horizontally. It bears very conspicuous, upright spikes of yellow flowers up to 60cm tall, with individual flowers to 4cm across. Leaves large and pinnate to 45cm long. Seed pods black when ripe, to 20cm long.

MILKWEED Malay: Bunga mas
Asclepias curassavica Apocynaceae
(Asclepiadoideae)
A larval food plant of the Common Tiger (p. 69).
These plants have milky latex in their tissues and
are toxic because they contain cardiac glycosides.
The caterpillars sequester the poisons from the
plant, which deters birds from eating them.
Introduced from tropical America. Often grown
in gardens but also now common growing wild.
A slender, upright herb to about 60cm tall. The
conspicuous bright red flowers occur in umbrella-
shaped bunches of 10–12 flowers at the top of
the stem. The five petals are folded downwards,
revealing the yellow corona. Narrow, dark green
tapering leaves to about 12cm long.

COCONUT PALM Malay: Kelapa
Cocos nucifera Palmae (Arecaceae)
The leaves provide food for the larvae of the Palm King (p. 100). The Coconut's natural
habitat is along the beaches of tropical shores as the coconuts containing the seeds float
and are dispersed by the ocean, sprouting wherever they land. Additionally, because of
their usefulness for coconut milk, coconut water, *gula melaka* (sugar from the sap), fibre,
thatch and timber, Coconuts are widely cultivated. Height to 20m, and pinnate leaves to
6m long in a terminal crown. The fruits (the coconuts) grow in clusters among the leaves
and make a dramatic thud when they drop.

Some Common Nectar Plants

SNAKEWEED Common Snakeweed **Malay:** Selaseh Dandi
Stachytarpheta indica Verbenaceae (verbena family)
A bushy, shrubby plant up to about 1 metre tall. The small, vivid blue flowers have five petals and are about 6mm across, and the corolla tube is 6mm long. They occur in long, thin upright spikes up to 25cm in length. A few flowers at the same height open each day and drop off in the afternoon, followed by more the next day. Leaves toothed, oval, up to 80mm long. *Stachytarpheta*, from Greek, means 'thicket of spikes'. Introduced from South America and now a very common flower of open, sunny places, found growing wild alongside paths and roads, and on waste ground in the lowlands. Highly attractive to butterflies.

CLERODENDRON Pagoda Flower **Malay:** Bunga Pawang (Magic Flower)
Clerodendrum paniculatum Verbenaceae (verbena family) > Lamiaceae (mint family)
A substantial, slightly branched and woody based shrub up to 3m tall. The distinctive, showy, conical flower head is composed of numerous small red flowers with long, slender tubular corollas. The long stamens projecting well beyond the petals create a feathery impression. The large, dark, three-lobed leaves have an unpleasant smell if crushed, whereas the flowers are scentless. Often planted as an ornamental in parks and gardens. Highly attractive to butterflies, especially the large birdwings.

IXORA Javanese Ixora **Malay**: Jarum jarum
Ixora javanica Rubiaceae (coffee family)
A large bush to 3m high. The numerous small flowers open orange, turning red later, and occur in large, flat-topped clusters at the ends of the branches. The corolla tube is narrow and up to 5cm long, culminating in four small petals spreading out flat. Leaves oval and up to 25cm long. The Bornean common name means 'needles', and refers to the shape of the flower buds before they open. Often grown in gardens as an ornamental, and sometimes used as hedging, it is in fact native to Borneo and Southeast Asia and is widespread as a wild plant, mostly in forest or along riverbanks, in semi-shade. Several other wild ixoras occur in the forest. Particularly attracts birdwing butterflies.

LANTANA [Prickly Lantana] **Malay**: Bunga tahi ayam
Lantana camara Verbenaceae (verbena family)
A low, straggling bush up to 1m high, with small, blunt spines and a curious pungent smell. The flowers are small, orange, pink or white, darkening as they age, and occur

in stalked, flat-topped bunches. The corolla forms a slender tube about 1.5cm long, culminating in five broad, short petals spreading out flat. Leaves are oval with toothed edges and a pointed tip, up to 7.5cm long and with conspicuous veins. A native of tropical America and planted as an ornamental, it has now spread to open, sunny sites in the lowlands, including roadsides and waste ground. Very attractive to many diverse species of butterfly.

Abang, Fatimah (2006), *Butterflies of Malaysian Borneo*, University Malaysia Sarawak, Malaysia.

Bascombe, M. J., Johnston, G. & Bascombe, F. S. (1999), *The Butterflies of Hong Kong*, Academic Press, London.

Bates, Henry Walter (2009), *The Naturalist on the River Amazon*, John Beaufoy Publishing Ltd, Oxford (first published in 1863).

Braby, Michael, F. (2004), *The Complete Field Guide to Butterflies of Australia*, CSIRO Publishing, Australia.

Chung, Arthur Y. C. (2014), *Discovering the Insects of Heritage Amenity Forest Reserve, Sandakan*, Sabah Forestry Department, Malaysia.

Corbet, A. S. & Pendlebury, H. M. (1934), *The Butterflies of the Malay Peninsula*, Kyle, Palmer & Co., Ltd, Kuala Lumpur.

Corbet, A. Steven & Pendlebury, H. M. (1956), *The Butterflies of the Malay Peninsula* (2nd ed.), Oliver and Boyd, Edinburgh/London.

Corbet, A. Steven & Pendlebury, H. M. (1978), *The Butterflies of the Malay Peninsula* (3rd ed.), Malayan Nature Society, Kuala Lumpur.

Corbet, A. Steven & Pendlebury, H. M. (1992), *The Butterflies of the Malay Peninsula* (4th ed.), Malayan Nature Society, Kuala Lumpur.

D'Abrera, Bernard (2006), *World Butterflies*, Hill House Publishers, Australia.

De Kok, R. P. J. & Utteridge, T. M. A. (2010), *Field Guide to the Plants of East Sabah*, Kew Publishing, Kew.

Ek-Amnuay, Pisuth (2012), *Butterflies of Thailand* (2nd ed.), Amarin Printing and Publishing Public Co., Ltd, Thailand.

Engel, David H. & Phummai, Suchart (2008), *A Field Guide to the Tropical Plants of Asia* (2nd ed.), Marshall Cavendish Editions, Singapore.

Enriquez, Major C. M. (2008), *Kinabalu – The Haunted Mountain of Borneo*, Opus Publications, Malaysia.

Fleming, W. A. (1975), *Butterflies of West Malaysia and Singapore*, Vol. 1, E. W. Classey Limited, England.

Flemming, W. A. (1975), *Butterflies of West Malaysia and Singapore*, Vol. 2, Longman Malaysia SDN. Berhad, Kuala Lumpur.

Ford, E. B. (1990), *Butterflies* (5th ed.), Bloomsbury Books, London.

Fox, Avril (1986), *Common Malaysian Moths*, Longman Malaysia, Selangor.

Glover, Beverley (2007), *Understanding Flowers & Flowering*, Oxford University Press, Oxford.

Hanbury-Tenison, Robin (ed.) (2010), *The Great Explorers*, Thames & Hudson Ltd., London.

Henderson, M. R. (1961), *Common Malayan Wildflowers*, Longmans, London.

Heywood, V. H., Brummitt, R. K., Culham, A. & Seberg, O. (2007), *Flowering Plant Families of the World*, Royal Botanic Gardens, Kew.

Hian, Steven Neo Say (2001), *Butterflies of Singapore* (2nd ed.), Singapore Science Centre, Singapore.

Holloway, J. D. (1987–2005), *The Moths of Borneo* (published in several parts), Southdene Sdn. Bhd., Kuala Lumpur.

Igarashi, Suguru & Fukuda, Haruo (1997), *The Life Histories of Asian Butterflies*, Vol. 1, Tokai University Press, Tokyo.

Igarashi, Suguru & Fukuda, Haruo (2000), *The Life Histories of Asian Butterflies*, Vol. 2, Tokai University Press, Tokyo.

Johnston, Gweneth & Bernard (1980), *This is Hong Kong: Butterflies*, Government Information Services, Hong Kong.

Kehimkar, Isaac (2008), *The Book of Indian Butterflies*, Oxford University Press, Oxford.

Khoon, Khew Sin (2010), *A Field Guide to the Butterflies of Singapore*, Ink on Paper, Singapore.

Kirton, Laurence G. (2014), *Butterflies of Peninsular Malaysia, Singapore and Thailand*, John Beaufoy Publishing, Oxford.

Monastyrskii, Alexander & Devyatkin, Alexey (2002), *Common Butterflies of Vietnam*, Labour & Social Affairs Publishing House, Vietnam.

Morrell, R. (1960, reprinted 1988), *Common Malayan Butterflies*, Longman Malaysia SDN, BHD., Selangor Darul Ehsan.

Newland, David, Still, Robert, Tomlinson, David & Swash, Andy (2010), *Britain's Butterflies*

▪ Bibliography ▪

(2nd ed.), Wild Guides, Hampshire.

Nijhout, H. Fredcrik (1991), *Development and Evolution of Butterfly Wing Patterns*, Smithsonian Institution Press, Washington and London.

Oates, Matthew (2011), *Butterflies: Spotting and Identifying Britain's Butterflies*, National Trust, United Kingdom.

Otsuka, Kazuhisa (1988), *Butterflies of Borneo*, Vol. 1, Tobishima Corp, Tokyo.

Otsuka, Kazuhisa, Seki, Yasuo & Takanami, Yusuke (1991), *Butterflies of Borneo*, Vol. 2, Tobishima, Tokyo.

Otsuka, Kazuhisa (2001), *Butterflies of Borneo and South East Asia*, Hornbill Books, Malaysia.

Owen, Denis (1980), *Camouflage and Mimicry*, Oxford University Press, Oxford.

Payne, Junaidi (1994), *This is Borneo*, New Holland Publishers Ltd.

Polunin, Ivan (1987, reprinted 2010), *Plants and Flowers of Singapore*, Marshall Cavendish Editions, Singapore.

Robinson, Gaden S., Ackery, Phillip R., Kitching, Ian J., Beccaloni, George W. & Hernández, Luis M. (2001), *Host Plants of the Moth and Butterfly Caterpillars of the Oriental Region*, The Natural History Museum, London.

Salmon, Michael A. (2000), *The Aurelian Legacy*, Harley Books, Colchester.

Schappert, Phil (2005), *A World for Butterflies*, Firefly Books, USA.

Shelford, Robert Walter Campbell (2012, first published 1916), *A Naturalist in Borneo*, Forgotten Books, Great Britain.

Shiew, Foo Tok (1986, reprinted 2002), *A Guide to the Wildflowers of Singapore*, Singapore Science Centre, Singapore.

Smith, Colin (2011), *Butterflies of Nepal*, Himalayan MapHouse, Nepal.

Tan, Horace & Khoon, Khew Sin (2012), *Caterpillars of Singapore's Butterflies*, National Park Board, Singapore.

Utteridge, Timothy & Bramley, Gemma (2014), *The Kew Tropical Plant Families Identification Handbook*, Kew Publishing, Kew.

Vane-Wright, Dick (2003), *Butterflies*, The Natural History Museum, London.

Waldbauer, Gilbert (2012), *How Not to Be Eaten*, University of California Press, California.

Wallace, Alfred Russel (2010, first published 1869), *The Malay Archipelago*, Beaufoy Books, Oxford.

Wickler, Wolfgang (1968), *Mimicry in Plants and Animals*, Weidenfeld and Nicolson, London.

Wijeyeratne, Gehan de Silva (2015), *Butterflies & Dragonflies of Sri Lanka*, John Beaufoy Publishing, Oxford.

Wong, K. M. & Phillipps, A. (1996), *Kinabalu Summit of Borneo*, The Sabah Society.

ARTICLES/PAPERS

Wallace, Alfred Russel (1867), 'Mimicry, and other protective resemblances among animals', Transcribed and edited by Charles H. Smith, PhD (2010).

Robinson, J. C., 'Swallow-tail butterflies of Sabah', *Sabah Society Journal*, Vol. VI, No. 2, 1975–76, Sabah Society, Kota Kinabalu, Sabah, Malaysia, pp. 5–22.

Houlihan, Peter, R. (2012), 'A guide to the butterflies of Sabangau', *The Orangutan Tropical Peatland Project*, Indonesia.

Holloway, Jeremy D. (1984), 'Notes on the butterflies of the Gunung Mulu National Park' (Part 6), *The Sarawak Museum Journal*, Vol. 30, No. 51, pp. 89–131.

Monaenkova, D., et al (2012, online). 'Butterfly proboscis: combining a drinking straw with a nanosponge facilitated diversification of feeding habits'. *Journal of the Royal Society Interface* 9:720-726

Robbins, R. K., 'The false head hypothesis: predation and wing pattern variation of Lycaenid butterflies'. *American Naturalist* 118: 770–775

▪ INDEX ▪

ACKNOWLEDGEMENTS

I would like to thank the many people who have helped and encouraged me throughout preparing the book: Cosmo Phillipps contributed a large number of photos and without his generous contribution it would have been impossible to complete the work. Quentin Phillipps organised all our field trips and read the first draft of the manuscript, contributing numerous useful suggestions. Caroline Bowman undertook the massive task of grading and labelling our photographs so that eventually the better ones made it into the book. Karen Phillipps for her numerous meticulous illustrations.

My thanks also to all the following: In Borneo – Anthea and Tony Lamb, who lent me many useful reference books, C K Leong and Roger Raja, who travelled with us on some trips, Stephen Sutton, Arthur Chung and Victor Hitchings, who generously shared their knowledge of local butterflies, similarly Jeremy Holloway. Anthony Chieng, Hanyrol H. Ahmad Sah and the staff at the Ulu Ulu Resort, Temburong, Brunei, Lawrence Chin, and the staff at Tabin Resort, Sabah, George Hong and the staff at Danum Valley Rainforest Lodge, Sabah, Robert Ong, and the staff at Sepilok, Sabah, Ose Murang of Penrissen Heights, Sarawak, Pak Agusdin, Sungai Wain, Kalimantan, Amir, Erwen, on Maratua, Kalimantan, Hans Dols and the Panaga Natural History Society, Brunei, Samson Sumaila, Moses, Chun Xing Wong, Shavez Cheema. Serena Lamb, Alex Lamb. John, Gina, and Rachel Hamilton. In UK – Fehmida Mohamedali, Mamta Kanal, Kate Harper, Monica Cornforth, Paul Gibson and Filipe De Sousa, Trish Beer, Clint Twist. John Beaufoy, Rosemary Wilkinson, Krystyna Mayer and Nigel Partridge, at John Beaufoy Publishing.